For Eleanor, her friends
and their families.

Published 2013 by
Bloomsbury Publishing Plc, 50 Bedford Square, London
WC1B 3DP

Copyright © 2013 text by Anne Harrap
Copyright © 2013 photographs as listed on p224

ISBN (print) 978-1-4081-8037-2
ISBN (e-PDF) 978-1-4081-8673-2
ISBN (ePub) 978-1-4081-8674-9

Page design and typesetting by Nimbus Design
Printed in China by C&C
Offset Printing Co., Ltd
10 9 8 7 6 5 4 3 2 1

The RSPB speaks out for
birds and wildlife, tackling
the problems that threaten
our environment. Nature is
amazing – help us to keep it
that way.

If you would like to know
more about the RSPB, visit
the website at www.rspb.
org.uk or write to: The
RSPB, The Lodge, Sandy,
Bedfordshire, SG19 2DL;
Tel: 01767 680551

Contents

Acknowledgments

The idea for this book was conceived with the help of family members and friends and I thank them all for being so supportive and for spending a considerable time with me out in the field, seeking out subjects for research and photography. I would like to specially mention the following because of their patience, support and hospitality: Teucer and Sarah Wilson and their children, Lily, Freyer and Arthur; Charlie and Helen Thurston and their daughter Isabel; Gwen Luker; Lenny and James Thomson and their children Charlotte, Rosie and Jimmy; Chloe and Dave Garramone and their daughter Gypsy-Kate; Nigel Redman and Cheryl Sifontes; Deborah and Andy Ward and their daughter Vicky; and Rick and Julia Barnes and their children Dan, Katie, Joe and Hanni.

My heartfelt thanks must go to Simon, my husband for being both chief photographer and companion on many forays into the wilds and a willing listener, and to our teenage daughter Eleanor, to whom this book is dedicated.

I would like to thank the many naturalists and photographers around the country who have helped the book along by recording and publishing their findings, enabling me to readily source reliable information and photographs: in particular, Martin Collier, John Walters, and Maria Fremlin.

Thank you to Lisa Treadwell for enthusiastically agreeing to engrave the Artist's bracket.

I must also thank the Bloomsbury Natural History department, especially Lisa Thomas – and Nicola Liddiard whose design brought the idea to life, for their help in the production of this book, which I hope will inspire a new generation of naturalists.

Foreword

The very first time you open a guide to British birds, or plants, or insects it can seem a bit daunting. How will you ever be able to recognise and identify such a fabulous diversity of organisms, especially when so many of them initially seem so similar? Surely this can only be a lifetime's work, something that will be near impossible to master. But no, actually it comes very quickly and even remarkably easily when you spend time out in the field down on your knees or peering through binoculars actively teaching yourself. Of course flicking through books or perusing the Internet may help but there is no substitute for the hard graft of working something out for yourself: it's then that you'll remember it – usually for the rest of your life.

This great book approaches such trials of recognition and familiarisation by making a quest out of it and by making it fun too. It sets you a target and is sure to set up competitions between friends and fellow budding naturalists. I imagine furious races to amass points and spot the choice species! Of course it takes all types of everything to make the natural world tick but whilst all organisms are equal – some are more equal than others. We all have lists of the things we would most like to see: some distant, some shy and some rare. And achieving encounters with these things is what drives the curious and determined naturalist on through wind, rain, traffic jams and near misses, it's what drives them all of their lives. So pick up this book and take up the challenge, get out into the wonderful wild world and start to collect some rich experiences and amazing views of beautiful plants and animals ... and the points they deserve. No cheating!

Chris Packham

The Great British Wildlife Hunt

Step out into the great British countryside and join wildlife enthusiasts across the country in the hunt for a fascinating selection of British wildlife. Look for 164 species of birds, mammals, insects, plants and fungi. Explore woods, heaths, wetlands, farmland and coast in the search for these plants and animals. Some are easy to find, some much harder. Each species has been given a skill value: the higher the number, the harder it is to find. To see all 164 species you will need to travel around the country and visit lots of great places. But, wherever you live, you can find a good selection nearby, and in the process you may discover hidden gems, places that you will want to visit again and again.

This book will show you how to work out: **Where to go**: to recognise the right habitats, the environments where your target species are likely to be found, and plan day trips and holidays to exciting new places. It gives tips on **When to Go**, to enable you to look for them at the right time of year and the right time of day. Share your experiences and sightings with others. You can challenge your family and friends to look out for each species too. Who is the best detective? Who is the best hunter, the most skilled observer? Who has the enthusiasm and the curiosity needed to stay out that little bit longer or go that extra mile to see something extraordinary? Let looking for wildlife to become part of who you are – your second nature – and you will soon be enjoying the natural world in a whole new way with this great family-friendly wildlife hunt.

How to use this book

Humans are by nature hunters and this book is all about hunting for wildlife – mammals, birds, reptiles, amphibians, fish, insects, ferns, flowers, trees and fungi. There are five sections: Woodland, Wetland, Heath and moor, Coast and Open countryside, all habitats that are found throughout the British Isles. Each section starts with an introduction to the habitat, followed by the species pages, which appear roughly in the order that the animal or plant that they cover is likely to be seen, with those resident all year at the beginning. The species pages tell you what to look for, where to go and when, as well as having some fabulous photographs and top tips.

Getting started

First select your target species and study the text and range map. Can you find a suitable location near to where you live, or will you have to travel further afield or perhaps even wait for a holiday in another part of the country? Familiarise yourself with its habitat and do some research. Look at a map to see if you can spot a likely place. Once you have decided where you are going, use the map to work out what sort of terrain you will encounter and to check for car parks and public footpaths. Decide how long you will stay: a short walk requires little planning but for a whole day's adventures you will need a picnic and perhaps some special kit. What else might you see? A good place for wildlife will often have several of the book's target species.

Be patient

Do remember that you won't see everything at once. As you become more familiar with the wildlife in the book you will realise that some things are much easier to find than others. And, even if you don't find your target species, you will always see something of interest (after all, this book covers only 164 animals and plants; there are thousands of others). It doesn't matter if you take a lifetime to see something, there will be lots of interest and enjoyment along the way. Indeed, that's the beauty of watching wildlife – there's always something new to see!

The scoring system

You can earn points for every species that you find. The more points, the harder it is to find. The easier species have just five points and will get you a Bronze medal. Silver is much harder, and Gold the hardest of all. Invent a day-trip challenge, a holiday challenge, a lifetime challenge or even a habitat challenge and record your successes in the back of the book.

20 The Great British Wildlife Hunt

30 The Great British Wildlife Hunt

50 The Great British Wildlife Hunt

How to look for wildlife

This book is all about observation, but if you don't know how to look, you will never 'see'. Everyone can get to know the basic habitats: woodland, marsh, farmland, but when you understand the building blocks of each habitat, the more you will be able to 'see' the wonderful wildlife on these pages.

Every habitat is made up of plants and animals living together in communities. Every plant and animal in each community has a different role to play (each occupies a particular niche). Learn to recognise these communities, and their major players (for example the trees, birds and butterflies in woodland), and you will soon be finding some of the less obvious members: the fungi, beetles and mosses.

HABITAT
Woodland A wide range of communities exist here.

COMMUNITY
Beech Tree Plants and animals that rely on the Beech.

NICHE
Wood Ant
Major predators, eating many insects, but also prey for other creatures.

COMMUNITY
Forest floor Plants and animals that rely on the ground layer.

NICHE
Fungi Responsible for decay and the recycling of nutrients.

Finding your way

MAPS Everyone, whether they live in the town or in the countryside, should own a good map of their local area. For day trips and holidays a map is essential. It can tell you where the footpaths, tracks, public rights of way and open access areas are, as well as nature reserves, country parks, car parks and picnic sites. Most importantly for wildlife hunting, a map will give information about habitats: woodland, heathland, marshy ground, rivers, streams and ponds, saltmarsh and cliffs are all marked.

Ordnance Survey (OS) maps have by far the best coverage of the British Isles, showing incredible detail, essential if you are hill walking and excellent in all terrain. The best maps for walkers are the OS Explorer series, at 4cm to 1km. OS maps are now available online for you to plan your own route (search for 'getamap'). Teach yourself how to use a map and compass, particularly for hill walking, and how to read a grid reference, which is useful for keeping a record of where you found your quarry.

New technology

There are lots of portable devices that can be of use to the wildlife watcher. Technology can fail, so never rely solely on these devices.

GPS Hand-held GPS units use satellites to calculate their position. They are great for recording the precise location of a sighting.

Smartphone Some are equipped with GPS and can display your location on a simple map. Phones are increasingly available with useful information, such as the nearest teashop or garage, but you do need to have good mobile coverage, so don't depend on them.

Satellite navigation (SatNav) Popular for in-car navigation, but few can accept an OS grid reference and a postcode can cover a large area in the countryside, so of limited use in locating the starting point for a walk.

Google Earth A bird's-eye view of terrain can be very useful when planning routes, and is especially useful in working out the habitats present, although small ponds and streams are usually invisible. The website wtp2. appspot.com/wheresthepath.htm, allows you to see an OS map alongside a Google Earth image, which is brilliant for studying the landscape before you visit or even when you are out and about if you have a smart phone and a mobile signal.

Kit

Once you have been out on a few wildlife hunts, used a map to find your way and, most importantly, found one or two target species, you may decide that your experience could be enhanced by carrying with you a few items of kit. These are my favourite items.

Camera Mobile and smart phones are a great start, as are compact digital cameras. Small and portable, they are at their best when taking photographs of stationary objects, including landscapes, and are especially good for close-up shots of small things. For anything that moves, however, a 'bridge' (mirrorless) camera or a digital SLR is a better bet, although heavier and more expensive, and these are the only real choice if you want to take really good photographs of birds.

Binoculars Some things are always just too far away! There are now some great, lightweight binoculars. Choose a pair with a magnification no greater than10x and check that they will focus on your feet – close-focus is great for seeing the details of butterflies and dragonflies.

Hand lens Essential for those real close-up moments. Hand lenses come in various magnifications but you will be best with 8x or 10x. Hold the lens as close to your eye as possible and move the object you are looking at inwards until it comes into focus. Once you have mastered the art you will see what a great piece of kit this is and will always want to have one with you. If you haven't got a hand lens, a magnifying glass is worthwhile, but they are bulkier and do not enlarge the image as much.

Pond dipping net and tray A must to see aquatic life close-up. A net with a square end is best in a river, while a rounded end works well in a pond. A wide white tray makes seeing your catches easy. Take this kit down to the coast as well for use in rock pools.

Small rucksack To carry your kit, plus water, picnic and of course, this book – make sure it has its own special place in your rucksack.

Don't become a slave to your kit – sometimes you may want to travel light and that's fine, because all that's really essential are your eyes and ears and a willingness to look.

Recording what you see

There is every reason to record what you see, for your own enjoyment and future reference. Taking notes on the spot is the best way of recording things accurately. Jot down details of the date, time and location (you could use an OS grid reference), time, weather conditions and what you saw – how much detail you include is entirely up to you. If you are handy with a pencil, make some sketches at the same time, and it is often useful to draw a simple map. When you get home you may want to write things up neatly in your own nature diary, either in book form or on a computer. You can also use the spaces on pages 214-221 to record the date and location that you first spot each of the species in this book.

> ## Smartphone apps
>
> More and more recording apps are being written for smartphones, allowing the user to record details of species, date and location on the spot and then transmit them to a computer or recording scheme.

Your records can also contribute to science and conservation. There are many national data-collecting schemes, and you can help these organisations to build-up a picture of the distribution of a plant or animal on a regional or national scale, to track the rise and fall of populations, or the spread of invasive species – all information vital to effective conservation. The following societies will welcome your records, and will often have details of specific surveys that you can join in with throughout the year:

* Mammal Society: *mammal.org.uk*
* BTO (British Trust for Ornithology): *www.bto.org*
* RSPB (Royal Society for the Protection of Birds): *rspb.org.uk*
* Buglife: *buglife.org.uk*
* Butterfly Conservation: *butterfly-conservation.org*
* British Dragonfly Society: *british-dragonflies.org.uk*
* Marine wildlife: *marlin.ac.uk*
* BSBI (Botanical Society of the British Isles): *bsbi.org.uk*

As well as the species in this book, you are likely to come across many others while out hunting. Don't forget to record these to build up a bigger picture. Take photographs too, make your own album or send your records and photos to our Facebook page *www.facebook.com/Wildlife.Hunt* where we will be building up our own picture of Great British Wildlife.

Happy hunting!

WOODLAND

British woodlands support some of Britain's best-known wildlife, but what you can find in a wood depends very much on what kind of wood it is. Learning to recognise the different types of woodland will really help you to know just what species to look for and where to look for them.

Once, about 10,000 years ago, the whole of Britain was covered in trees. Brown Bears, Wolves, giant cows (called Aurochs), Moose and horses roamed and mighty trees fell, creating clearings where smaller shrubs and wild flowers grew until tree saplings filled the spaces once more. Early humans entered the scene clearing more spaces, creating fires and hunting and gathering. Little changed for several thousand years but gradually, due to human land clearances it came to the point where only 5 per cent of the countryside was wooded, though today that has increased to 11 per cent.

Happily some woodlands – known as ancient woods – remain on the same sites. The trees may have been cut down and re-grown many times, or the woods managed for timber and firewood, but these woods with their unbroken history, are still some of the very best places to go to find woodland wildlife – minus the bears and Wolves of course!

How to spot an ancient wood

To identify the jewels in the crown of British woodlands, look for these features:

Irregular boundaries This can show that the woodland existed before the surrounding field patterns took shape. More recently planted woodlands tend to have straight edges. Look carefully at woods on an OS map and try to find old maps where important woods were named individually: Great Wood and Home Wood are typical names.

Undisturbed soils Ancient woodland sites have some of the least disturbed soils in Britain, never having been ploughed or artificially drained or fertilised. No wonder they are the best places to look for fungi, mosses and wild flowers.

Old trees and dead wood Not all ancient woods have very old trees; many may have been cut down, but look for woods with trees of a variety of ages, including some older trees, and look for mossy, decaying tree stumps too.

Human management Timber and coppice were once very valuable commodities. To stop deer from nibbling the young shoots and people helping themselves, a bank and ditch were often built around a wood, with a fence on top. These banks and ditches are often still visible and help to tell the wood's story.

Broadleaved woodland

Broadleaved or deciduous trees drop all of their leaves in the autumn and remain leafless over the winter. Examples include English Oak, Beech and Ash, trees that make up some of our best-loved woodlands. An oak wood, with an understorey of coppiced Hazel (see p.19) seems timeless, as if unchanged for centuries and is home to a wide variety of wild flowers, birds and insects. Beech is native to the southern half of Britain and its canopy casts a deep shade, below which a Beech wood is characteristically open; its towering grey trunks and rich autumn colours are well-loved by many people. The deep leaf litter of a Beech wood is great to explore for fungi and interesting plants. Ash woods are found more often in northern Britain and on limestone and chalky soils. Ash has a much lighter canopy than Beech and its leaves may not open until June, so many more plants can grow in an Ash wood.

Woodland trees and shrubs

Trees and shrubs form the framework of a wood and have a big impact on the variety of other plants and animals to be found there.

Get to know the common trees of British woodlands. Some have characteristic shapes, or distinctive bark and twigs, but for the beginner the shape of the leaves and the presence of distinctive flowers or fruits are the most helpful features.

English Oak
The common oak in southern and eastern Britain. Acorns are borne on long stalks.

Sessile Oak
The common oak in northern and western Britain. Acorns are almost stalkless.

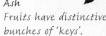

Ash
Fruits have distinctive
bunches of 'keys'.

Beech
A stately, tall, smooth-barked tree;
in the autumn the fallen beechmast
attracts a variety of birds.

Hazel
Usually found as a
shrub; in the early spring
catkins or 'lamb's-tails'
are very conspicuous,
followed by hazelnuts in
the autumn.

Rowan
Leaves rather like those of Ash,
but the leaflets are toothed.
Produces sprays of white flowers
in spring and bunches of
bright red berries in autumn.

Sycamore
Thought to have been introduced
in the 16th century, it spreads
easily via its winged seeds and
can 'invade' ancient woodland.

Field Maple
Most are hedgerow shrubs but
given the chance grows into an
attractive tree. The leaves are
lobed and resemble miniature
Sycamore leaves.

Sweet Chestnut
Probably introduced by the
Romans, the delicious fruits
are a favourite for all foragers.

Coniferous woodland

Conifers have needle-like leaves. Most are evergreen and shed their leaves throughout the year rather than dropping them all in one go in the autumn. The ground beneath conifers is often carpeted with fallen needles and sometimes little else can grow there. Most conifers also produce their seeds inside hard, woody cones. Around 57 per cent of the UK's woodlands are made up of conifers, but only three species are native: Scots Pine, Juniper and Yew.

Yew

Juniper

Plantations

Everyone is familiar with conifer plantations – formal rows of trees in angular, often straight-sided blocks – a complete contrast to the native Caledonian pine forests. Plantations can be found right across Britain and dominate some upland areas. They contain a range of conifers: Scots and Corsican Pines, Norway and

Scots Pine

Caledonian pine forest

The most extensive natural coniferous woodland in Britain is the Caledonian pine forest of Scotland, with Abernethy Forest the largest remaining stand of native pinewood. Majestic old Scots Pines, covered in mosses and lichens, give cover, food, and nest sites and their trunks with overlapping plates of bark provide nooks and crannies for a huge range of invertebrates. Other native trees include birches, willows, Rowan and Aspen, and the ground is carpeted with Juniper, Heather, Bilberry and a variety of exciting wild flowers.

To see some of Scotland's fantastic wildlife you must visit these forests. What you find could be as simple as the imposing atmosphere and resinous scent of the trees; it could be the nests of busy wood ants amongst the pines (p.26), or Red Squirrels scampering in the branches (p.24), and this is where to look for Crested Tit (p.22).

Sitka Spruces and various firs, while in some places deciduous trees are planted in rows along the edges as a disguise. Plantations of trees grown as a commercial crop have been around for more than 200 years, but the foundation of the Forestry Commission in 1919 resulted in a huge increase in the area planted. Many plantations have good public access for walking, cycling and other outdoor pursuits, and some are now managed with wildlife in mind – sunny spots may produce some nice surprises, such as Wood Wasps (p.49) or wood ants (p.26).

Mixed woodland

Commercial plantations may have a mixture of coniferous and broadleaved trees – in the period after the Second World War many ancient woodlands were felled and largely replanted with conifers, leaving just a few deciduous trees. On the larger farms and estates mixed woodland was planted not just for its timber, but also for its landscape value, or as cover for Pheasants. Whatever its origins, mixed woodland is often good for wildlife, and is the place to look for Firecrest (p.41).

New and amenity woods

Woodland can grow on land that was once something else such as farmland. Birchwoods often spring up on heathland and dunes for example – look here for the colourful Fly Agaric (p.64). In addition, in recent years completely new woods have been planted, often for amenity and recreation. New woods, whether natural or planted, may have a good variety of trees, both native and exotic, but it will take many decades (or longer) before they support the diversity of wildlife to be found in ancient woodland. Nevertheless, they often have open access and are well worth exploring, as a selection of the more mobile plants and animals will be quick to move in.

Where to look – the structure of woods

A wood can be divided into several, easily recognisable layers that, once learnt, can help you to locate specific plants or animals.

The canopy
The branches and leaves at the top of the trees that receive much of the available sunlight. Viewpoints and towers can provide a glimpse of canopy life – look for singing birds and especially for Purple Hairstreak butterflies (p.54).

The shrub layer
Shrubs such as hawthorn, willow, Holly, Ivy and bramble are found here as are saplings and the lower branches of the larger trees. The dense cover provides places for birds to nest and, along the edges of rides and clearings, song posts, and sunny spots for insects such as Common Darter (p.51).

Field layer
The layer occupied by wild flowers. Look for Wood Sorrel (p.40), Bluebell (p.44), Toothwort (p.39) and woodland orchids. The amount of light available varies according to the time of year – most woodland flowers bloom in spring, before the leaves appear on the trees – and the type of tree: Ash lets in more light than Beech.

Ground layer
The domain of dead wood, fallen leaves and branches and soil is where, especially in damp woods, you will find mosses and liverworts (p.65), and fungi such as Fly Agaric (p.64). This is also the place to look for Lesser Stag Beetle (p.50).

Coppicing

Most deciduous trees will grow again (coppice) from the base if they are cut down – the coppice stool (cut stump) forms buds and several shoots are produced. This is the basis for the age-old woodland management scheme known as coppicing. A variety of trees, but especially Hazel and Ash, were cut on a 10 to 15 year rotation, and the harvest of timber provided poles for construction and tools as well as wood for charcoal. Unintentionally, coppiced woodland is brilliant for wildlife and many woods are now managed again as coppice by conservation bodies.

When the trees are first felled the extra light reaching the woodland floor encourages the growth of wild flowers, while insects thrive in the sunshine. After three or four years the growing shoots form an impenetrable thicket. Wild flowers become shaded out and bees and butterflies withdraw but the coppice is now suitable for nesting birds – warblers, thrushes and Nightingales. After several more years the shoots become long poles and unsuitable for nesting but are ready to be cut and the cycle begins again. In well-managed coppice the wood is divided up into compartments and cut in rotation to provide a continuous supply of wood, so there is always a variety of habitat. Walk around until you have found each stage and notice the differences for yourself.

A woodland diary

You can visit woods all year round, and in fact the seasons are spelled out for you in a woodland; Bluebells, the first green leaves, the dawn chorus of spring, the deep shade and sunlit glades of summer, the fungi, leaf colour, and busy birds and mammals of autumn and the bare bones and quick glimpses of winter.

February to June The best times for breeding birds.
March to June Most woodland plants will be in flower.
June to September Butterflies and other insects.
September to January Autumn colour, as well as fungi, mosses and liverworts.

The Great British Wildlife Hunt

10

Ancient tree

Truly majestic, often with massive gnarled branches: you will never forget your first encounter with an ancient tree, especially if you give it a hug.

Watch for bats emerging at dusk.

Holes in the bark – good for nesting birds especially owls, tits, Nuthatches and Treecreepers, and small crevices for spiders, beetles and woodlice.

Large holes around the roots are good hiding places for Stoats and Weasels.

LOOK FOR Fabulously shaped trees with really broad trunks. Look for holes or large crevices in the trunk and many stunted or dead branches, which may be covered in fungi, lichens, mosses and ferns. Many of the oldest trees will have multiple branches and a short trunk, having been cut in the past for their timber. To get a rough idea of the age of a tree such as oak, Beech, Sycamore or Sweet Chestnut, measure the distance around the trunk at chest height. A rough guide is that every 2.5cm of the circumference equals a year, so a tree with a girth of 250cm will be about 100 years old. Aim to find a tree with a girth more than 4m or even 6m for a really ancient oak.

WHEN TO GO All year round. In winter, the twisted shapes of the branches help to give character to our historic landscapes.

WHERE TO GO Ancient trees can be found in ancient woodland and old hedgerows, but are most obvious (and often most impressive) when they grow singly in the parkland of big estates, large town parks, large gardens and churchyards – all great places to seek out your 'giant'.

TOP TIP ⋆ Depending on the species, ancient trees attain a larger or smaller girth as they grow old. Test with a hug – one hug will go around an old Silver Birch, or a hug with elbows touching for a Hawthorn – but take care, the thorns are sharp.

The Great British Wildlife Hunt

10

Witches' broom

These wild-looking twiggy growths on the branches of birch trees are not made by witches; they are usually caused by a parasitic fungus.

Silver Birch

LOOK FOR An uncontrolled mass of twiggy growths, up to 100cm across, on the branches, often weighing down the stem when they are near the tip. The smaller clusters resemble birds' nests. There may be just one on a tree or many, and they can be high in the trees, so use your binoculars for a closer look. The twiggy growths can be covered in mosses and lichens and make great habitats for invertebrates and feeding places for woodland birds. From a distance could be mistaken for Mistletoe, but this has green leaves and is rarely found on birches.

WHEN TO GO Visible all year round, but most obvious in winter when the leaves have fallen.

WHERE TO GO Found throughout Britain. There are two species of native birch, and both may be bewitched: Silver Birches are commonest on light, sandy, acid soils, especially mixed woodland around the edge of heaths. Downy Birch prefers damper habitats, usually woodland on heavy soils and beside rivers. Hornbeam, a close relative of birches, may also be attacked by the fungus.

HORNBEAM

NEWS EXTRA! Witches' brooms start off as a mass of small buds on the branch or trunk of a tree. These expand into twiggy growths producing small leaves on which the fungal spores grow and are dispersed.

The Great British Wildlife Hunt

30

Crested Tit

A cheeky and charismatic small tit, it can be seen flitting fast around the branches and trunks of Scots Pines in the beautiful Caledonian pine forests in Scotland.

Length 11.5cm.

LOOK FOR The black and white crest is obvious and gives this bird such a happy and inquisitive expression it cannot be mistaken for any other. Watch Crested Tits feeding acrobatically amongst the pine needles and cones in the trees, very much like other members of the tit family.

WHEN TO GO A resident breeding bird and present all year round, pairing up from February to May.

WHERE TO GO Restricted to pine forest in northern Scotland, both in the remnants of the ancient Caledonian pine forests and more modern plantations of Scots Pine. In winter they may forage in nearby low scrub and heather. Many places, from bird reserves to cafés, now provide bird feeders that attract both Crested Tits and Red Squirrels.

TOP TIP ★ Crested Tits often feed high in the canopy so listen out for their calls – a few high-pitched notes and a distinctive soft, purring trill. Knowing the common calls of Coal, Blue and Great Tits will help you pick out a Crested Tit.

The Great British Wildlife Hunt

10

Jay

The most striking and colourful member of the crow family, a Jay can be noisy and obvious, or surprisingly hard to see.

Length 34cm.

Broad wings with blue wingbar and white rump obvious when bird is in flight.

LOOK FOR Although noisy, Jays are shy and restless birds, rarely staying still, so it can be quite hard to have a good view. On the ground they tend to hop and jump about rather than walk or run. You'll usually hear a Jay before you see it – the alarm call is a harsh, unattractive screech.

WHEN TO GO A bird of deciduous woodland, oak woodland is the Jay's preferred habitat. It is also found in hedgerows, parks and gardens, especially in the autumn and winter, but never far from trees.

WHERE TO GO Jays are most obvious in the autumn as they fly back and forth collecting acorns. Each bird collects around 5,000 acorns through the autumn and can carry several at once, filling its gullet and carrying one in its bill. It then flies a kilometre or more from the oak tree before burying the load. These acorns are then retrieved and eaten over the winter months. Jays can be quiet and secretive when nesting.

SCIENCE STUFF
THE STUNNINGLY BEAUTIFUL WING FEATHERS CAN OFTEN BE PICKED UP, HAVING FALLEN FROM A MOULTING BIRD. BIRDS HAVE INCREDIBLE EYESIGHT AND GOOD COLOUR VISION, AND EXPLOIT VISUAL SIGNALS IN DISPLAY AND SPECIES RECOGNITION, WHICH IS WHY SO MANY BIRDS ARE COLOURFUL.

The Great British Wildlife Hunt
25

Red Squirrel

Red Squirrels are adorable. Try and visit the Scottish Highlands to see their incredibly acrobatic antics, which will always make you smile.

Smaller than the Grey Squirrel, with bushy ear tufts in winter.

LOOK FOR Red Squirrels scamper around with quick movements and scolding and chattering calls. They build twiggy nests ('dreys') close to the main trunk of a large tree. Other telltale signs are scratch marks on bark and clusters of discarded, stripped pine cones, split nut shells and chestnut husks in heaps on the ground.

WHEN TO GO Active all year round. In summer they are most active during the early morning and evening, but they are busy all day when the young are freshly out of the nest. In winter the late morning is the best time to see them. In very bad weather Red Squirrels will shelter in their dreys.

WHERE TO GO Most – around 75 per cent – of Red Squirrels are found in the Highlands of Scotland or the woodlands of the Isle of Wight. Seek out large areas of Scots Pine forest or mixed woodland with many pine trees. Check out the feeders in visitor hot spots: various nature reserves, tea rooms and other visitor attractions put out food for them and you can be rewarded with great views.

TOP TIP ★ Take binoculars to see them well.

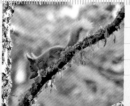

Grey Squirrel

The Great British Wildlife Hunt

5

Although they are easily seen in gardens and parks, try to collect your points for Grey Squirrels in a more natural habitat as well.

LOOK FOR Fast and agile, Grey Squirrels make their twiggy dreys high in a fork or close to the trunk of a tree. They have two litters each year, with lots of activity and scolding *chuk-chuks* around the nests. Grey Squirrels eat almost anything: feeding signs are discarded pine cones or hazelnuts on a tree stump and shredded Sweet Chestnut husks on the woodland floor. A commotion of bird calls can be a sign that a squirrel is after eggs or young.

Never have long ear tufts

Grey but with some brown patches, especially on the head.

WHEN TO GO Active all year round, they can be seen on a daily basis in gardens and parks. In more rural woodlands they are most visible on mild days in the autumn and winter.

WHERE TO GO Almost anywhere with trees: deciduous, mixed and coniferous woodland, and parks and gardens of all sizes in both town and the countryside.

NEWS EXTRA! The Grey Squirrel is not a native species. It was introduced from the USA from 1876 onwards and is considered a pest of forestry. It is also thought to be responsible, one way or another, for the decline of the native Red Squirrel.

The Great British Wildlife Hunt

10

Red Wood Ant & Scottish Wood Ant

The largest of all British ants, these are highly social animals, so take time to watch them at work. Their nests can be in the same place for years and you can return to them again and again.

There can be more than 250,000 ants in one nest.

Worker ants are about 10mm long, while the queen can be up to 17mm.

LOOK FOR Their unique nests, which are up to two metres high and made up of pine needles and tiny wood fragments. Most of the ants that you see are workers, which are black and dull orange. They are effective predators and constantly move to and from the nest to forage for invertebrates for their young, while they feed themselves and their queens on honeydew, a sugary liquid taken from aphids high in the tree canopy.

WHEN TO GO The nests can be seen all year round, but the ants are only active from February to late October. Look for the large copper-coloured queens in April and May and watch for the winged males and queens leaving the nest to mate in June and July.

WHERE TO GO Established coniferous woods on sandy and peaty soils, especially along the edges of clearings and tracks that catch the sun. The Red Wood Ant is confined to England and Wales, while the Scottish Wood Ant is found in Scotland, northern England and Wales.

TOP TIP ★ Be wary near to an active nest as they can be very feisty and will be over your feet and up your legs in no time. They spray formic acid from their rear ends – it is uncomfortable but usually harmless, although the smell can be quite pungent. Some birds visit ants' nests just to be sprayed with formic acid, which wards off pests in their feathers – a behaviour known as 'anting'.

The Great British Wildlife Hunt

15

Bracket fungi

These fungi form shelf-like projections, the 'brackets', on the trunks of living and dead trees. They come in a variety of colours, shape and sizes, and have some great English names.

TURKEYTAIL

OYSTER MUSHROOM

CHICKEN OF THE WOODS

BEEFSTEAK FUNGUS

LOOK FOR More or less flat fruiting bodies, usually without a stalk, attached to fallen twigs or larger branches on the woodland floor, or to standing stumps and tree trunks. These 'brackets' can be large or small, occur singly or be attached in horizontal or vertical rows. Some are annual and disappear after the spores have been released, while others can last for many years. They are usually found on dead or dying wood, but only certain species actually cause the death of their host tree.

WHEN TO GO Present all year round. Bracket fungi look their best after wet weather, with some only appearing after mild, damp weather in the autumn.

WHERE TO GO Anywhere there are large trees – woodland, parks and large gardens.

TOP TIP ✳ Look out for the Artist's Bracket, which is very hard with pale spores beneath. You can draw a picture on it! © LISA TREADWELL

The Great British Wildlife Hunt

25

Roe Deer

This small, elegant deer was hunted to extinction in England by 1800 but clung on in Scotland. It was re-introduced to England from Scotland and Germany in the 19th century and happily is still increasing its range.

75cm tall. The black nose stands out.

Only the males have antlers.

LOOK FOR A medium-small deer, chestnut brown in summer but greyer in winter, always with a black 'dipped in ink' muzzle and white rump patch. Look for regular runs or tracks through long grass and for the droppings, which are slightly larger than a Rabbit's. Roe Deer make loud barks and will stamp their feet if disturbed.

WHEN TO GO Present all year. Roe Deer are easiest to see at dawn and dusk but can be seen at any time during the day. From April to June they are often seen on field edges, eating the growing crops, and males are territorial during the rut (when they compete for females) from mid July to mid August.

WHERE TO GO Roe Deer occur in all types of woodland, including young plantations, birch thickets and scrub. Look along rides, in clearings and other open areas, and in nearby grassland and crops.

NEWS EXTRA! Often solitary, but you may see females with young, from May onwards. More commonly seen in groups in winter, or in areas where numbers are high.

Treecreeper

A rather unobtrusive woodland bird but with definite character. Spot one on a tree trunk and delight in its busy behaviour.

Length 12.5cm, with a long bill and long tail.

LOOK FOR An active bird with a very characteristic habit: it flies to the base of a tree trunk and climbs upwards in a spiral around the trunk, using its tail for support, probing cracks and crevices in the bark for food with its fine, down-curved bill. Its movements are sometimes jerky, but at other times it seems to creep stealthily. The bird's calls are thin and high-pitched, the song is a full warble that falls in pitch and has a final hurried flourish (a bit like a high-pitched Chaffinch).

WHEN TO GO Resident year-round, rarely straying far from the breeding area, but most obvious in winter when the leaves have fallen from the trees. Treecreepers often join noisy parties of tits and other birds.

WHERE TO GO Deciduous, coniferous and mixed woodland, with plenty of large trees, especially those with a rough bark.

SCIENCE STUFF

TREECREEPERS MAKE USE OF GIANT SEQUOIA TREES, WHICH ARE OFTEN PLANTED IN LARGE PARKS AND GARDENS, ROOSTING IN HOLLOWS THAT THEY DIG OUT OF THE INCREDIBLY THICK BARK. TAKE A TORCH AND LOOK FOR A LINE OF FEATHERS NESTLING IN A CREVICE – THEY WILL RETURN NIGHT AFTER NIGHT.

The Great British Wildlife Hunt
10

Great Spotted Woodpecker

You will love the striking black, white and red coloration, but its eerie drumming, echoing through spring woodland, makes this woodpecker special.

Male has red on nape.

Length 23cm, a little bigger than a Starling.

Broad wings and striking red under the tail.

Nests in tree holes.

LOOK FOR The striking plumage and undulating, flapping and gliding flight. Look for old tree stumps and rotten branches that have been pulled apart and holes in trees. Watch them searching a tree trunk for their prey, wood-boring insect larvae, moving steadily upwards then swooping off to the next tree. Often attract attention with loud *kik* calls. Stand quietly and listen for the drumming noise in spring.

WHEN TO GO Present all year round. Drumming can be heard from late winter to spring. In mid to late summer, after the breeding season, they can be harder to spot.

WHERE TO GO Anywhere with plenty of mature trees and standing dead wood: deciduous, coniferous and mixed woodland; copses; hedgerows with tall trees; parks and gardens. Will visit bird feeders.

TOP TIP ＊ Drumming is produced by the bill repeatedly hitting a branch or trunk, which acts as a sounding board. This drumming helps to attract a mate and to announce its territory.

The Great British Wildlife Hunt

20

Nuthatch

Always sleek, with never a feather out of place, the Nuthatch would win a fashion contest with its cool, blue-grey back and contrasting pale orange underparts.

Length 14cm, the same as a Great Tit, but looks bigger.

LOOK FOR Distinctive jerky movements, noticeable as it walks up and down tree trunks. The Nuthatch is the only British bird that can climb down trees headfirst. Listen out too for the loud, whistled calls and the audible tapping as it splits open a nut that it has wedged into a crack in the bark.

WHEN TO GO Present all year round, rarely moving far from their breeding sites. Most obvious in early spring, when they can be very noisy, and when feeding young.

WHERE TO GO Deciduous woodland and parkland with large, old trees, less commonly in mixed woodland and occasionally gardens. They particularly like woods with Beech, oak, Hazel, Sweet Chestnut and Hornbeam, which provide them with winter food, and will visit bird tables for peanuts.

SCIENCE STUFF

THE NUTHATCH HAS EXTRA LONG CLAWS THAT ENABLE IT TO GRIP THE BARK FIRMLY AND EVEN WALK ALONG UPSIDE DOWN. IT NESTS IN HOLES IN TREES, AND IT IS WORTH CHECKING THESE OUT WITH BINOCULARS, AS THE NUTHATCH PLASTERS THE ENTRANCE WITH MUD TO MAKE IT JUST THE RIGHT SIZE.

The Great British Wildlife Hunt

15

Lichens

Lichens are a fascinating combination of two different types of organism that live together: a fungus, which provides a sheltered home, and a food-producing alga.

LICHENS COME IN MANY DIFFERENT SHAPES AND SIZES:

Crusty & scaly

Thin, flat crusts on rocks, branches or soil. Especially common on old walls and gravestones.

Leafy

Usually some broad raised lobes spreading out from the base.

Shrubby

Shrubby lichen may be stalked, with red fruiting bodies; shrubby, looking like tangled branches, or bearded, wispy growths dangling from trees.

WHEN TO GO One great thing about lichens is that they look the same all year.

WHERE TO GO Lichens occur throughout Britain, in almost any habitat: rocky outcrops, old concrete, the bark of trees, even bare soil. The older and less disturbed the habitat, the more species you are likely to find – old walls and churchyards are great places to look – but they are sensitive to pollution, so you may find only a few species in cities. Lichens indicate clean air.

Lasallia pustulata, a leafy lichen. This common upland species has long been used by people for dyeing and as a survival food – 'Rock Tripe'!

TOP TIP ★ There are more than 1700 species in Britain so unless you want to become an expert, just enjoy their variety and what they can tell us about the environment.

Oak apple gall

A gall is an abnormal growth caused by another organism living in or on the host plant. With over 1000 different galls in Britain, it is good to be able to recognise at least one.

A female wasp will lay eggs in a bud.

Up to 5cm in diameter – roughly the size of a golf ball.

LOOK FOR Pinkish-red, spongy, apple-like growths appear where the buds should be in the twiggy branches of an oak tree. Later in the year they are brown and harder, looking more like paper and feeling more like cork. The grubs inside the gall pupate in the summer and the winged adults chew their way to the surface, leaving small holes to mark their departure.

WHEN TO GO Oak apple galls are particularly visible from the end of May until July. They may remain on the twigs throughout the following winter.

WHERE TO GO Deciduous woods and mature hedgerows where there are oak trees.

NEWS EXTRA! Different species of gall wasp produce different galls, and on the same oak tree you may find these other common galls.

The tiny wasps emerge in June and July.

Marble gall Brown, marble-shaped and very hard.

Spangle gall Each protects a tiny larva.

The Great British Wildlife Hunt
10

Long-tailed Tit

These tiny birds are busy, sociable, and chatty, staying together almost year-round in family groups as they flit through the bushes and trees.

LOOK FOR A ball of fluff with a long tail. The plumage is an unusual combination of black, white and pink. Often attracts attention with its calls, a thin, *tsee-tsee-tsee*, a fuller *tup, tup*, and rippling trills: *tsirrup, tsirrup*.

The body is tiny, just 5cm long, but the tail is 9cm long.

WHEN TO GO Present all year. They gather in family flocks most of the time and can be very visible and noisy in winter, calling to one another as they move from tree to tree.

WHERE TO GO Anywhere with plenty of trees and shrubs – deciduous and mixed woods, copses, parks and gardens. Long-tailed Tits have recently taken to visiting bird tables and feeders.

NEWS EXTRA! From late winter, look for pairs busily nest building. The nest is often built in spiky vegetation such as Common Gorse, hawthorn or Blackthorn and is a real work of art. A ball of moss, cobwebs and hair, it is well camouflaged on the outside with up to 3,000 flakes of lichen. They gather around 1,500 small feathers to line the interior.

Polypody

A common fern, but easily overlooked. Once you have learnt to recognise its fronds, polypody will surprise you with the diverse habitats in which you see it.

The Great British Wildlife Hunt • 15

Fronds variable size, but up to 60cm in length. There are three species, but they are hard to tell apart.

LOOK FOR The fronds (leaves) are thick and leathery with a short stalk. They are shaped like a herringbone and taper gently towards the tip. The scientific name *Polypodium* means 'many-footed' and relates to the stems, which creep through the soil, bark or wall, the leaves emerging at intervals.

WHEN TO GO In leaf for most or all of the year, with new fronds appearing mid- to late summer. The spores are produced in autumn and winter.

WHERE TO GO Deciduous woodland, growing on the ground (often on old banks), on mossy stumps and even as an epiphyte on trees in suitably damp and humid environments. Also found growing on sand dunes, sea cliffs, limestone pavements, and stone and brick walls, often in full sun.

SCIENCE STUFF

FERNS REPRODUCE VIA SPORES AND THE STRUCTURES THAT PRODUCE AND PROTECT THE SPORES (THE 'SORI') CAN BE SEEN ON THE UNDERSIDE OF THE FROND IN LATE SUMMER. THEY ARE BRIGHT ORANGE WHEN MATURE, AND THE YELLOW SPORES ARE DISPERSED BY THE WIND.

The Great British Wildlife Hunt

15

Sparrowhawk

Fast and furious, it relies on surprise to catch its prey when hunting. A superb raptor, perfectly adapted to the woodland environment.

Males are much smaller than females (male 28cm long, female 38cm).

In flight note the broad wing and long, squared-off tail.

LOOK FOR A small, broad-winged, long-tailed bird of prey soaring lazily high above a wood or copse, sometimes in pairs. When Sparrowhawks are hunting, you may only get a brief view: they fly rapidly along rides, across clearings and along hedgerows, periodically jinking from one side of the hedge to the other or changing direction as they try to surprise small birds.

WHEN TO GO Present all year. The soaring display flights can be seen above the woods from late February onwards. Nesting pairs tend to be rather secretive.

WHERE TO GO Any deciduous, coniferous or mixed woodland. Some remain around nesting territories all year, but in the autumn and winter others spread out into farmland and they will also visit garden bird tables, hoping to catch thrushes, tits, finches, sparrows and even pigeons.

TOP TIP ✳ A hovering bird of similar size will always be a Kestrel.

The Great British Wildlife Hunt

10

Chiffchaff

A small, rather drab warbler but with a big voice. One of the first warblers to sing in spring, frequently from an obvious perch, the song from which it takes its name is easily recognised.

Around 11cm long, the Chiffchaff is not much bigger than a Wren.

LOOK FOR An attractive, very active bird flitting around the ends of branches and flying out to pick up an insect. Listen for the unmistakable song as it repeats its name over and over again from the top of a tree, *chiff-chaff, chiff-chiff-chaff ...* , with a somewhat irregular rhythm. At other times it remains in thick cover.

WHEN TO GO Small numbers of Chiffchaffs spend the winter in southern Britain, but most are summer visitors, arriving from early March and leaving for a Mediterranean winter by October. Chiffchaffs are very vocal in the early spring, and can be heard singing at any time of the day.

WHERE TO GO Breeds in deciduous and mixed woodland, copses, tall hedgerows, commons and large gardens, especially where bushy, thick undergrowth is combined with large trees to perch in when singing.

WILLOW WARBLER

SCIENCE STUFF

UNLESS SINGING A CHIFFCHAFF IS HARD TO SEPARATE FROM A WILLOW WARBLER, ALTHOUGH IT IS DULLER, WITH BLACKISH LEGS AND FEET (REMEMBER 'THE RIFF-RAFF ALWAYS HAVE DIRTY LEGS').

The Great British Wildlife Hunt
15

Speckled Wood

The creamy speckles on the velvety brown wings of a basking Speckled Wood mirror the dappled sunlight and deep shade of its woodland home.

Males and females look similar.

LOOK FOR Males of this distinctive butterfly are obvious as they search and compete for mates along a stretch of woodland ride or hedgerow. Look for them sitting on low vegetation or patrolling their chosen patch, circling upwards when two or more meet. They mainly feed on aphid honeydew high in the canopy but also visit flowers and are especially fond of ripe blackberries in the autumn.

WHEN TO GO The flight period extends from late March to October in southern Britain, with peaks in May and June and again in August and September.

WHERE TO GO All types of woodland, hedgerows, gardens and parkland with plenty of trees. The female lays eggs on grasses along sunny paths, but they can be found throughout a wood, even in deep shade.

SCIENCE STUFF

HONEYDEW IS THE SWEET, SUGARY LIQUID PRODUCED BY APHIDS. THE APHIDS FEED BY SUCKING UP PLANT SAP, BUT USE JUST A LITTLE OF THE SUGARS IN THE SAP FOR THEIR OWN NUTRITION, BEFORE MUCH OF THE REST IS EXCRETED AS HONEYDEW.

Toothwort

An amazing, truly parasitic plant; the stem and flowers are entirely pinkish-white! It has no need for chlorophyll as its host plant provides all the energy that it needs.

LOOK FOR The ghostly white flowering stems of Toothwort grow straight from the ground and have rose-pink flowers all turned to one side. It is easily overlooked when growing amongst Wild Garlic and Wood Anemone, both of which flower at the same time, and you will have to look carefully amongst the stems and leaves of these plants.

WHEN TO GO Late spring. The flowers appear in April and May, sometimes even earlier, usually before the leaves open on the trees above.

WHERE TO GO Deciduous woods, old hedgerows and copses on damp, rich soils, often close to the banks of a river or stream. Hazel is the commonest host, but it is worth checking beneath a variety of trees.

NEWS EXTRA! It is the seedpods, which resemble rows of white teeth in a jaw, that give the species its name. This is an uncommon plant: send your records to your local plant recorder (page 222). It is an easy plant to photograph, as it is sturdy and does not move much in the wind.

The Great British Wildlife Hunt

15

Wood Sorrel

With its fresh green leaves and nodding white flowers, Wood Sorrel is a delightful plant, whether it carpets the ground under Hazel coppice or hugs the moss-covered roots of an ancient tree.

The white flowers have delicate lilac veins.

LOOK FOR Nodding white flowers held above soft, three-lobed, clover-like leaves on long, delicate stalks.

WHEN TO GO In flower from March to May. Curiously, there is a second flowering of closed, self-pollinating petal-less flowers in autumn.

WHERE TO GO Deciduous or mixed woodland, sometimes even coniferous woodland. It carpets the ground in favoured habitats. Look for the plants on shaded banks, in deep, leafy soil at the base of trees, amongst tree roots and growing over moss-covered logs and rotting branches.

COMPANION PLANTS OFTEN SEEN GROWING CLOSE BY.

MOSCHATEL

WOOD ANEMONE

SCIENCE STUFF

THE LEAVES FOLD BACK AND THE PETALS CLOSE UP AT DUSK, IN BAD WEATHER OR DURING HOT SUNSHINE TO PROTECT THE FLOWER, MAKING THE PLANT LOOK RATHER DIFFERENT.

Firecrest

The Great British Wildlife Hunt

40

This relative newcomer to Britain is dazzling, and often number one in a birder's 'Top Ten'. Springtime woodland walks have taken on a whole new interest as the chances of seeing this tiny bird increase.

Length only 9cm.

'Cross'-looking facial expression.

Fanastic bronze shoulders.

LOOK FOR A tiny bird, rather like the much commoner Goldcrest, but brighter, with a black line through the eye and a bold white eyebrow. Male Firecrests show off their vivid orange-red and yellow crown dramatically when displaying in the spring. The call, thin and high pitched is very like a Goldcrest's but the song, a high-pitched, rhythmic, *tsi-zi-zi-zi-zi-zi-zi-zi-zi* that gets a little louder towards the end, lacks the up-and-down rhythm of a Goldcrest and is often the best way to find a Firecrest.

WHEN TO GO Firecrests are resident in central and southern England and south Wales, and spring visits to typical habitat may reveal displaying and singing birds. Others arrive from Europe in the autumn and winter, especially around the coasts of southern Britain, and often join roaming flocks of tits.

WHERE TO GO Coniferous woodland, especially stands of Norway Spruce, but you can also find them in mixed woodland. In winter Firecrests will visit scrub, parks and large gardens.

NEWS EXTRA! Once just a rare migrant, Firecrests first bred in England in 1962. They slowly increased over the next 40 years, but the breeding population then took off and there may now be more than 1,000 pairs.

The Great British Wildlife Hunt

20

Woodcock

The Woodcock's ghostly, nocturnal habits and cryptic camouflage have endowed it with an aura of mystery. Check out any suitable habitat on your spring and summer evening walks.

Length 34 cm – looks smaller than a Wood Pigeon in flight.

This sort of view is rare and requires great patience!

LOOK FOR The aerial display flight, known as 'roding', when a Woodcock flies in a wide circuit around its territory. You will usually first notice the distinctive call: a thin, far-carrying *tissik*, interspersed with a frog-like *wark-wark-wark* that you will only hear when the bird is close overhead. A Woodcock will then suddenly appear, flying just above tree height, as a characteristic silhouette with the long bill pointing downwards. It is very hard to see one on the ground, as they are so well camouflaged, but you may flush one by accident – it will fly up fast and erratically and disappear rapidly.

WHEN TO GO Woodcocks display on spring and summer evenings from around 30 minutes before sunset. In the autumn Woodcocks come to Britain from the continent and, following a 'fall', may be found almost anywhere.

WHERE TO GO Damp woodland, both deciduous and coniferous, with plenty of open spaces, or a mixture of woodland, bog and heathland. In hard winter weather, especially when there is snow on the ground, they can sometimes be seen feeding out in the open in the fields and even flushed from back gardens.

TOP TIP ✶ When listening for Woodcocks (or any other bird) cup your hands around your ears while keeping your mouth open and you will increase your hearing by about 40 per cent. Try it – it really works!

Bird's-nest Orchid

A hauntingly addictive plant: once you have found a group of Bird's-nest Orchids you will always be looking for them beneath the gloom of a beech tree's canopy.

Around 30cm tall.

Up close the flowers have a sweet, sickly smell.

No green leaves.

LOOK FOR The honey-coloured stems of Bird's-nest Orchids are hard to spot as they emerge from the leaf litter in the darker, shadier parts of a wood, especially on days when the sun filters through to the ground. Once you have found one, look around, the chances are there will be many more.

WHEN TO GO Flowers from May to July, although the previous season's dead stems can often be found year-round. Warm, wet springs encourage flowering and in dry years there may be none at all.

WHERE TO GO Anywhere with stands of Beech, especially over chalk and limestone, from Beech woods, where it may be the only plant growing beneath the trees, to mixed deciduous woods and ancient hedgerows.

SCIENCE STUFF
BIRD'S-NEST ORCHID IS COMPLETELY DEPENDENT ON FUNGI FOR ALL ITS NUTRIENTS, SO ONLY OCCURS WHERE FUNGI GROW. ITS TANGLE OF ROOTS, HIDDEN UNDERGROUND, GIVE IT THE NAME 'BIRD'S-NEST'.

NEWS EXTRA! May be mistaken for Yellow Bird's-nest, which is a similar colour and also parasitic on fungi. Its flowers droop when fresh and only stand upright when seeds form.

The Great British Wildlife Hunt · 15

Bluebell with Early Purple Orchid

The magnificent sight of thousands of Bluebells covering the floor of an ancient woodland, on view for just three weeks of the year, is difficult to beat.

Early Purple Orchids have boldly spotted leaves and can be up to 45cm tall.

LOOK FOR Bluebells occur by the million in 'bluebell woods' and are too well known to require description, but you will often have to look carefully to see the purple spikes of the orchids amongst them.

WHEN TO GO Bluebells flower from early April in the south to late May in the north, before the leaves are on the trees. They have a delicious scent, strongest on a calm, warm evening. Flowering at the same time, the Early-purple Orchid is one of the first wild orchids to appear in the spring.

WHERE TO GO Bluebell woods can be found up and down the country, but Early-purple Orchid is a bit fussier, preferring deciduous woodland, mainly of ancient origin and chalk or limestone. Look where the canopy is more open to find both species together: clearings, rides and coppiced areas.

NEWS EXTRA! Native Bluebells bear nodding flowers all on the same side of the spike. The pollen on the anthers is creamy-white.

The Great British Wildlife Hunt
25

Wood Warbler

This little bird's bright green and lemon yellow plumage echoes the colours of a springtime wood, and it also has a dazzling song.

LOOK FOR A small, active bird, flying out from branches to catch insects on the wing or acrobatically searching amongst the branches and leaves. The green upperparts and yellow throat and breast, clearly set off from the white belly, separate the Wood Warbler from Willow Warbler and Chiffchaff.

WHEN TO GO A summer visitor, arriving in late April and early May and leaving for tropical Africa in July and August. It is most obvious when newly arrived as the males are singing and establishing territories.

WHERE TO GO Open woodland with a high canopy and little or no undergrowth, often on slopes. Commonest in Sessile Oak woods in the uplands of the west of Britain, occasionally in Beech woods or mixed woodland with birch and Sweet Chestnut, but it has declined recently in the lowlands, where it is now rather scarce. Nests are built on the ground and are so well camouflaged they are rarely seen.

NEWS EXTRA! The song is glorious, a stuttering series of sharp, loud 'zip' notes that accelerates into a fast trill – the bird's whole body shakes as it reaches its crescendo. The song may be given in a parachuting display flight. Sometimes this trilling song is mixed in with a series of clear, whistled 'piu' notes. Just sit, watch and listen.

The Great British Wildlife Hunt

25

Longhorn moths

The males of these small moths have astonishingly long antennae and are incredibly entertaining to watch – you will be looking out for them everywhere.

GREEN LONGHORN

MEADOW LONGHORN

There are 15 species, all well worth looking out for. Most are scarce in Scotland.

Wing length varies from 5 to 11mm.

The antennae really are long!

YELLOW-BARRED LONGHORN

LOOK FOR Trees and shrubs bathed in sunshine, around which the males appear to dance; the movements of their antennae can be obvious. The colours of some catch the light and these tiny moths can look like bronze or gold jewels.

WHEN TO GO These common, day-flying moths are on the wing from early May and June. Pick a warm day; they are often obvious in the late afternoon sunshine.

WHERE TO GO Deciduous woodland, mature hedgerows, commons and some gardens. Some species congregate on the lower leaves of trees such as oak, Hazel and Rowan, others fly higher up.

NEWS EXTRA!

The swarms of males in spring can appear like little fairies fluttering in the sunlight – they are even known as fairy moths.

The Great British Wildlife Hunt

20

Wild Strawberry

Find your local patch of **Wild Strawberries** and harvest the plentiful tiny, sweet fruits. The seeds have been found in Neolithic excavations – evidence that our ancestors enjoyed them too.

The fruits are only 1cm across.

LOOK FOR A low creeping plant with glossy leaves, each divided into three leaflets. It produces rooting runners and may form large patches. The small, white daisy-like flowers appear on the end of thin stems and are followed by the nodding red strawberries. These fruits are much smaller than garden strawberries, and the seeds sit on the surface rather than being sunk into the flesh.

WHEN TO GO The white flowers are produced from April through to midsummer. The red fruits follow the flowers, and are sweetest and most delicious when in an open spot and well ripened by the sun.

WHERE TO GO Deciduous or mixed woods, particularly along rides and in open glades, also hedgebanks and verges. Grows on a range of soils, but likes those that are light and dry.

NEWS EXTRA! The Barren Strawberry grows in similar places. The leaves are blunter and a dull rather than a glossy green and if you look closely the petals are clearly separated at the base. As its name suggests, it does not produce edible red fruits.

The Great British Wildlife Hunt
40

Nut Weevil

A bizarre-looking creature, the female Nut Weevil has a snout of elephantine proportions. She uses it to bore holes into growing hazelnuts, in which she lays a single egg.

The snout and body length together total about 1cm.

The male's snout is much shorter.

LOOK FOR Diligent searching is required to find this beetle, hence the high score. Look for hazels and search amongst the leaves to find young nuts, which are pale green and soft – there may be female weevils lurking nearby. On sunny days it is also worth looking at hawthorns and other shrubs for adult weevils feeding on the flowers, and later in the year looking for fallen hazelnuts and examining them for exit holes.

WHEN TO GO Adults are active from April to September, but are mostly seen from May to August. Like many beetles they fly on warm evenings, and they may be attracted to lights.

WHERE TO GO Anywhere with Hazel bushes that are uncut and so are able to flower and develop nuts. Old oak woodland with Hazel coppice is a good place, as are tall hedgerows.

SCIENCE STUFF

THE FEMALE GNAWS A HOLE IN THE NUT AND LAYS A SINGLE EGG. THE HOLE THEN CLOSES AND THE LARVA EATS AWAY AT THE NUT. WHEN THE NUT FALLS, THE MATURE LARVA CHEWS ITS WAY OUT AND PUPATES IN THE GROUND, EMERGING AS AN ADULT THE FOLLOWING SPRING.

Giant Wood Wasp

Despite its appearance, this is a completely harmless insect. Its name comes from its wood-eating larvae. Watch the female laying eggs in a pine trunk – awesome.

The female has the long ovipositor, 1cm long. Males are all black and less likely to be seen.

LOOK FOR A large insect resembling a Hornet, but it is much more slender with long yellow legs and antennae and the obvious needle-like ovipositor. You may see the female quietly and determinedly hunting around, looking for a mate or for suitable trees to lay her eggs. The female drills into the timber with her ovipositor and is often seen in this position. The larva produces tunnels in the wood, up to 30cm deep.

WHEN TO GO Adults fly from May to October on warm, sunny days.

WHERE TO GO Wood Wasps are nearly always found in coniferous woods or mixed woods that have plenty of pine trees. Find sunny clearings, and woodland rides with piles of cut pine timber or fallen trees. The adults hatch out after up to three years living in timber as larvae, which is why you may have most luck around cut timber or in a timber yard!

SCIENCE STUFF

GET EXTRA POINTS FOR FINDING THIS LARGE ICHNEUMON FLY. SHE HUNTS FOR THE LARVA OF THE WOOD WASP AND WILL LAY HER EGG NEAR TO OR IN ITS BODY, DEEP WITHIN IN THE TIMBER. SHE HAS AN EVEN LONGER OVIPOSITOR THAN THE WOOD WASP'S FOR THE JOB.

50

The Great British Wildlife Hunt 45

Stag Beetle & Lesser Stag Beetle

The largest British beetle, the male Stag Beetle has jaw-droppingly huge antlers. It is often confused with the smaller, but also impressive, Lesser Stag Beetle.

FEMALE

Male Stag Beetles can be up to 7cm long, the females 5cm.

MALE

Stag Beetle

LOOK FOR Males are unmistakable. Females are smaller but have the same glossy brownish-black colouring. Large, fresh, holes in rotting stumps may mean that adults have recently emerged and could still be close by.

Lesser Stag Beetle

LOOK FOR Large and usually slow moving, thus easy to observe when found. Look around rotting timber for its holes and for wood shavings.

FEMALE

MALE

WHEN TO GO From May to September. The beetles can be found at any time of day but fly around looking for mates early and late in the day and even after dark.

WHERE TO GO Deciduous woods, parks and gardens with large old trees and lots of rotting stumps. Both species are commonest in south-east England as they prefer warm, dry conditions. London's suburbs are some of the very best places to spot a Stag Beetle, colliding with windows and even crash-landing in the street!

NEWS EXTRA! Stag Beetle is an endangered species and national surveys take place to monitor their fortunes. This creative 'habitat' – a 'loggery' in a country park – has been built to attract them.

The Great British Wildlife Hunt

10

Common Darter

One of the smaller dragonflies, the Common Darters' red and gold coloration mirrors the early autumn days when they can be very numerous, often well away from any pond.

Males have orange-red abdomens, while females and immatures are yellowish to light brown.

Eyes reddish-brown.

Wings held forward at rest.

LOOK FOR A small, reddish dragonfly. Restless, they are prone to fly out from a favourite perch and return again and again. Look for them on vegetation and also on fence posts, barbed wire, twiggy branches and sunny spots on the ground. They are commonly seen paired 'in tandem' as they lay eggs in suitable ponds.

WHEN TO GO On the wing from mid-June to the first frosts of November – the longest flight period of any British dragonfly – and they will fly in cooler conditions than many other species.

WHERE TO GO Common Darters breed in ponds, lakes and slow-moving sections of rivers and canals. They can also be seen regularly in woodland rides and clearings.

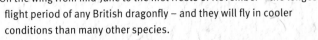

NEWS EXTRA! The Ruddy Darter shares the same habitat but is smaller, much redder and has a 'pinched-in' abdomen that looks almost club-shaped.

Enchanter's Nightshade

These tiny flowers seem to illuminate the otherwise dark places in which they grow. It has acquired one of the most romantic English names of any wild plant.

30–60cm tall.

Tiny white flowers.

LOOK FOR Tiny pinpricks of white flowers amongst the woodland shade in summer, often the only plant flowering at this time. The well-spaced flowers protrude delicately from a spike on top of large, green leaves. They may sometimes show a pink tinge, either from the visible stamens (pollen-producing structures) or the buds.

WHEN TO GO Flowers from June to September. The leaves are visible from April and persist with the seeds into November.

WHERE TO GO Deciduous woods and other damp shady places on hedgebanks and along streams and rivers, often forming large, spectacular patches.

SCIENCE STUFF

THE PLANT HAS AN EFFECTIVE METHOD OF DISPERSAL: THE SEED HEADS HAVE HOOKED BARBS AND ARE GOOD AT ATTACHING THEMSELVES TO ANIMAL FUR – AND YOUR CLOTHES, A GREAT EXAMPLE OF 'ZOOCHORY' OR ANIMAL DISPERSAL. ENCHANTER'S NIGHTSHADE ALSO HAS CREEPING ROOTS THAT SEEM TO BE INDESTRUCTIBLE!

The Great British Wildlife Hunt
25

White Admiral

This exotic butterfly is often seen gliding gracefully up and down sunny woodland rides. Its striking black and white markings attract attention.

Wingspan around 6cm.

Male and female look very similar. The colour of the underside of the wings is very different to the upperside.

BRAMBLE

HONEYSUCKLE

LOOK FOR Bramble flowers in the sunshine, along rides, in clearings and on the woodland edges. Brambles produce lots of nectar and are a great favourite. The females only lay eggs, however, on Honeysuckle leaves that are out of the sun, so look for the females in cool, shady places.

WHEN TO GO Visit on sunny days from late June to the middle of August.

WHERE TO GO Search out deciduous or mixed woodland in the south of England. They are also found in large gardens and parkland with plenty of woodland. The White Admiral is expanding its range northwards, so it is worthwhile looking for it in new areas too.

TOP TIP ✶ Puddles or even damp patches are a source of water and minerals. White Admirals often visit these and they are great places to try for a photo.

The Great British Wildlife Hunt

40

Purple Hairstreak

This butterfly scores highly because it is difficult to spot, although once you know where and when to look, the chances of spotting a colony are high.

LOOK FOR Small dark butterflies flitting around the branches high in the canopy. They fly up and then land again as they search for mates and honeydew. In dry spells you may be lucky to see Purple Hairstreaks at low levels searching for nectar.

WHEN TO GO Adults are on the wing from early July to early September (up to three weeks later in the north of England and Scotland). There is only one generation a year. Warm, calm, sunny evenings may prove to be especially successful.

WHERE TO GO Woods, parks, and hedgerow trees. Colonies are always found in oaks, both English Oak and Sessile Oak, and can even be found in a single isolated large tree. The colonies are usually high in the canopy, where the main food of the adult butterflies is aphid honeydew (see page 38).

TOP TIP ✳ You will need binoculars to get a good view. Try to find a good vantage point where the canopy can be easily seen. You may be rewarded with a display of the whole colony dancing above the treetops.

Slime mould

They may not be top of your most wanted list but these fascinating, brightly coloured organisms will charm even the most squeamish once you get to know them.

DOG VOMIT SLIME MOULD   COD ROE SLIME MOULD   PINK PEARL OR WOLF'S MILK SLIME MOULD

LOOK FOR The commonest and most obvious slime moulds look like patches of yellow or white sponge, plastered over a log or spilt on the ground. Neither animal, plant nor fungus, slime moulds are colourful, extraordinary and downright bizarre. They can even *move*. More remarkable, they can move *through* the soil or even *through* a log (although slowly), engulfing bacteria as they go. If you can, go back each day to track their progress.

WHEN TO GO All year after any warm, damp spell, but spring and autumn are the best times to look.

WHERE TO GO Damp shady places in deciduous woodland. Look on tree stumps, the tops and undersides of logs, particularly when very rotten, and on soft pulpy wood and piles of leaves.

SCIENCE STUFF

ONCE THOUGHT TO BE FUNGI, SLIME MOULDS ARE NOW PUT INTO THE GROUP 'MYCETOZOA', BUT THEIR EXACT RELATIONSHIPS TO OTHER ORGANISMS ARE STILL UNCLEAR. THEY HAVE TWO DISTINCT PHASES: A MOBILE FEEDING PHASE THAT IS ALMOST ANIMAL-LIKE, AND A STATIONARY REPRODUCTIVE PHASE THAT IS MORE PLANT-LIKE (LOOK CLOSELY WITH A HAND LENS AND YOU MAY SEE SOME BEAUTIFUL SPORE-PRODUCING STRUCTURES). THEY ALSO HAVE A SINGLE-CELLED PHASE THAT FEEDS UNSEEN IN THE SOIL AND ROTTING WOOD.

The Great British Wildlife Hunt
50

Bird's-nest fungus

A truly amazing find! Fungi are a fabulous group of organisms to study, but it is hard to think how and why Bird's-nest Fungi evolved, seemingly just to give us so much pleasure.

Field Bird's-nest 1–1.5cm tall.

Fluted Bird's-nest 1–1.5cm tall.

LOOK FOR Very small but instantly recognisable, the fruiting body looks like a tiny tumbler inside which the round spore sacs resemble a clutch of bird's eggs. The Fluted Bird's-nest can occur in large clusters, but there may be only one or two Field Bird's-nests together, making it much harder to find.

WHEN TO GO Fresh fungi are found from August to December, but the clusters of 'nests' may be recognisable for a long time and be found all year.

WHERE TO GO Damp places where there is moss and rotting dead wood. Check also well-rotted sawdust resulting from woodland management and, although associated with deciduous woodland, they may turn up in any undisturbed rotten wood, even urban flower beds mulched with wood chips.

SCIENCE STUFF

BEFORE THE FUNGI ARE MATURE, THE MOUTH OF THE 'NEST' IS COVERED OVER. THE COVER TEARS OPEN WHEN RIPE TO REVEAL THE 'EGGS' INSIDE.

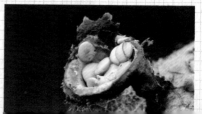

The Great British Wildlife Hunt

10

Stinkhorn fungus

The Stinkhorn, living up to its name, produces one of the most unforgettable smells you will experience in any woodland. You won't forget the sight of it either.

Up to 20cm high.

The 'eggs': these are the first signs of a Stinkhorn erupting from the ground.

The Dog Stinkhorn Fungus grows in similar places, but is smaller and richly coloured.

LOOK FOR Or rather smell – a rather sharp smell resembling rotting meat. Once you have the smell in your nostrils the fungus won't be too far away, perhaps hidden under bracken or brambles but sometimes out in the open. Its stem is stark white and the tip white when fresh but brown or black when ripe with spores. Usually occurs singly but there may be many scattered around suitable places.

WHEN TO GO August to October, but may be found from June in wet summers.

WHERE TO GO Occurs throughout Britain. Mature deciduous, coniferous or mixed woodlands where there is a good supply of humus-rich leaf litter.

NEWS EXTRA! You may spot flies, mostly bluebottles, buzzing around the fungus, attracted by the smell. When completely ripe, the tip turns black and the spores become a sticky goo, and cling to the flies' feet.

Fly Agaric

On warm, damp autumn days these striking fungi appear as if by magic. They are often found in 'troops' under favoured trees.

LOOK FOR The fungus starts off as an all-white dome that expands to form a bright red cap with varying amounts of raised white spots. The red fades to orange as it ages and the cap opens out flat.

Cap 8–20cm across, stem 1–2cm wide and 8–18cm high.

WHEN TO GO August to November. Warm, humid weather encourages all fungi to fruit, but they may be scarce in dry periods.

WHERE TO GO Deciduous, mixed or coniferous woods with a mixture of Silver Birch and pine, usually on acidic, sandy soils. Fly Agarics are also found under trees on heathland.

TOP TIP ★ This fungus is POISONOUS. Get down on the woodland floor to have a close look, take photographs or sketch it, but leave it undamaged for others to enjoy. TAKE CARE: The toxins in poisonous fungi cannot be absorbed through the skin, but you may put your hands to your mouth after touching them, so always wash your hands after a 'fungus foray'.

20

The Great British Wildlife Hunt

Mosses, liverworts & filmy ferns

These three groups of primitive plant can easily be mistaken for one another. Mosses and liverworts are found everywhere, but filmy ferns are real specialists. Score 20 points for each.

FILMY FERN

MOSSES

LIVERWORTS

3–10 cm long. Tiny ferns with fine, wiry stems and translucent fronds, each segment with a fine midrib. Just two species in Britain.

The leaves are spiralled around the stem, usually have a midrib, and are never lobed. Around 700 species in Britain.

The leaves are lined up in straight rows, never have a midrib and are often lobed. Around 300 species.

WHERE TO GO Mosses occur everywhere, but the greatest numbers and variety are found in damp, shady places: the woodland floor, tree trunks, rotten logs and stream-sides. Liverworts are also widespread, but are more restricted to damp places. Filmy ferns like it really wet and are a speciality of the north and west. They grow on tree trunks, rocks and banks in sheltered, shady places, often near streams in deep river gorges, wetted by waterfalls and springs.

WHEN TO GO Filmy ferns, mosses and liverworts are visible all year round, but mosses and liverworts are often more obvious in winter, when they are actively growing.

NEWS EXTRA!

The range of forms shown by mosses and liverworts is astounding. These are two of the commoner species.

Star-headed Liverwort

Silver-moss

HEATH & MOOR

Heaths and moors are truly wild and beautiful places that explode with colour when the heathers are in flower from July to September. Like ancient woodlands, these are landscapes that exude a sense of human history. A visit at any time of year, even when it is cold and bleak, will allow you to soak up some of their incredible atmosphere. Not surprisingly, their wildlife is also very special.

Special habitats

Similar but different, Heathland and moorland exist because of a special combination of soil, climate and human history. Both have a mixture of heathers, gorse, Bracken and rough grasses, making them easy to recognise, and both are found on poor, thin, acid soils. Heathland is mostly found on dry, sandy or gravelly soils in the lowlands of the south and east of England. There is often lots of bare ground, ideal for a variety of insects, and for snakes and lizards. Moorland is mostly found in the wetter parts of Britain in the north and west, often on peaty soils, and is a much damper habitat.

History

Both heathland and moorland are man-made habitats. Both started life when the first farmers cleared forests to create farmland. This took place as long ago as the Bronze Age or even earlier, perhaps 4,000 to 5,000 years ago. Their poor soils were quickly exhausted, however, and the land was no longer suitable for growing crops. Instead, it was given over to grazing animals – sheep and cattle. Together with the collection of firewood, the cutting of Bracken and gorse for bedding and feeding animals, and the occasional fire, grazing prevented the trees from returning for thousands of years. This great expanse of time has resulted in the heathland and moorland that we see today, allowing the development of rich communities of special plants and animals that rely on open, sunny, nutrient-poor habitats.

Heathland

Throughout history, heathlands have been steeped in mystery and intrigue. The constantly changing weather, sometimes scorchingly hot, often windy, sometimes still, perhaps misty, and cold in winter, together with nocturnal birds with strange calls ... it is no surprise that poems and stories of poachers and highwaymen abounded. Heathlands were often termed the 'bad lands' or 'wastes' and were rarely used for recreation. Today, however, much heathland has open access and the many birds, flowers, reptiles and insects can be enjoyed by everyone.

Some common plants of heathland and moorland

Heather Often dominates large areas. Individual flowers rather small and pale, appearing Aug–Sep.

Bell Heather Common, with bell-shaped rich pink flowers. Usually the first heather to flower, Jul–Oct.

Cross-leaved Heath Fairly common, usually in wetter areas. Dusty-pink bell-shaped flowers and grey-green leaves.

Bilberry A low, woody shrub, commonest in the north and west. Produces edible black berries. Known as blaeberry in Scotland.

Common Gorse Common and very spiny. Flowers all year, but most spectacularly Apr–May, when its coconut scent can be overwhelming.

Western Gorse Confined to W Britain and E Anglia. Just 1–1.5 m tall, and only flowers in late summer, alongside heathers, making a spectacular display.

Moorland

Characteristic of the wilder parts of Britain, moorland has a rugged beauty all of its own.
The typical terrain is a mixture of wet, tussocky grass, sheets of Heather and gorse,
and open boggy pools and streams, with just a few trees and stone walls to break the
monotonous wind. Moorland is home to Red Grouse (p.68), Short-eared Owls (p,67),
Golden-ringed Dragonflies (p.78) and, in some places, Heath Spotted Orchids (p.77).

Bogs

Both heathland and moorland are associated with bogs.
Bogs are areas of waterlogged ground, often dominated
by sphagnum mosses, with the wettest areas marked
out by the cotton-wool-like heads of Cottongrass. On
moorland in areas with high rainfall, where it is very wet,
blanket bogs may develop – the bog literally blankets
the ground over large areas. Even in the drier south and
east, some heaths have bogs in the low-lying valleys,
forming long, narrow strips of wet ground. Bogs are
always great places to look for interesting plants and
animals, but be careful – you could lose your wellies
(or worse).

Typical bog plants

*Cottongrass In mid-summer
the fluffy white seedheads
of Cottongrass can really
wow all those Pennine Way
walkers and stop them in
their tracks.*

*Sphagnum moss The
cushions of this moss can
carpet areas of very wet
ground and the great variety
of colours create beautiful
vistas, especially in autumn
and winter.*

Acid grassland

Much of a heath or moor may be covered by grass. As well as these grassy areas being easier to access (they are much less prickly than gorse) they often have areas of bare ground and Rabbit holes, where a number of small flowering plants and intriguing beetles and wasps can be found.

Common plants of acid grassland

Sheep's Sorrel *A common plant which is stunning when covering the ground in summer, when the whole plant turns red.*

Purple Moor-grass *Forms dense tussocks. It is the flowers that are purplish and the whole plant turns a rich ochre in autumn turning the moorlands gold.*

Conservation

Sadly, as fewer and fewer people lived off the land, heaths and moors were no longer valued for their harvest of Bracken, firewood or Rabbits and became easy targets for development and 'improvement'. Large areas of heathland have been ploughed up and converted to farmland. In other areas, heaths were simply abandoned and taken over again by trees, as both heathland and moorland rely on continued management by man to stop them reverting to woodland. The net result is that the area of heathland in Britain has shrunk greatly over the last 200 years.

Moorland too has not been without its problems. Most moorland is still grazed, mostly by sheep, but the number of animals has increased, causing overgrazing

Rabbit warrens

The Rabbit was introduced to Britain in medieval times to provide both meat and fur. The sandy soils of Breckland in south-west Norfolk and north-west Suffolk were perfect for them and a thriving industry produced many thousands of Rabbits each year.

Lakenheath Warren, in Suffolk was one of the largest, often producing over 100,000 Rabbits a year – a harvest that only ended when a military airbase was built over part of the warren in the Second World War.

of the heather, which eventually disappears, while many areas have also been drained to encourage more productive grassland. In other places large expanses of moorland have been planted with alien conifers. Because of these changes, some areas of moorland have lost much of their special interest for the wildlife watcher – you will now usually find the special

wildlife of the moors on the heather clad-slopes high above the lower grasslands.

The heaths and moors that remain are increasingly valued as special places for wildlife. Many are managed by conservation bodies such as the RSPB and the Wildlife Trusts. The traditional sight of grazing animals in the New Forest is spreading to other heaths – grazing by ponies, sheep or cattle helps to stop the succession to woodland. To protect what is left, the more people who get to know and love our remaining heaths and moors the better.

Finding heathland and moorland

Unless you are lucky enough to live near to a heath or moor, you will need to know how to find a good area. Both habitats are found throughout Britain, although by no means in every county. Use a map and look for the symbols for Heath and Moor. Their location will tell you what sort of habitat you will find; in the uplands, with the contour lines close together, many streams and rocky outcrops, the vegetation is likely to be moorland (and there may be clues in the name: upland moors are also known as 'fell', 'moss' or 'low'). In lowland Britain, on cliff tops, or on level ground with shallow valleys, you are likely to encounter heathland. The map symbols for scrub, mixed woodland or plantations may be shown close by, giving you a really good idea of the surrounding habitats. Sometimes there are clues in the name; such as Shepwick Heath in Dorset. Areas known as 'commons' may also be heathlands, such as Thursley Common in Surrey.

Both heathland and moorland tend to be wide open spaces with only scattered trees, so they can be windy and hot in summer with little shade, and cold in winter. They can be large areas to explore so if you're planning a day trip, be prepared with a picnic, water, suitable clothing and footwear and a compass. As your explorations may take you away from well-walked areas, don't forget a map (although there are often many paths and tracks that are not marked on maps, so keep a careful track of where you are).

The Great British Wildlife Hunt
15

Stonechat

This colourful small bird is one of the real characters of heaths and moors. It is often fairly tame as it flits from one vantage point to another, but use binoculars to get great views of this stunner.

The male has a black head and orange breast.

12.5cm long, roughly the size and shape of a Robin.

The female is browner above, with a duller breast.

LOOK FOR In spring, Stonechats are often found in pairs, perched on the top of adjacent gorse bushes or rocks, flicking their wings and tail. The male performs a dancing song flight, giving a short phrase that is a mixture of both high-pitched and scratchy sounds.

WHEN TO GO Present in Britain all year, although the breeding and wintering areas may differ. Easiest to see in spring and summer.

WHERE TO GO Stonechats breed on lowland heaths with plenty of gorse bushes, and in other scrubby grassland,

particularly near the coast. They also breed on heather moorland in the uplands, especially where there is some scrub, and in young conifer plantations. In winter they are usually found near the coast.

Gorse bushes are ideal nest sites.

TOP TIP ✶ When the birds are not obvious, listen out for the call that gives them their name – *chack, chack-chack* – the sound of two stones being knocked together.

Short-eared Owl

With its long wings and beautiful, haunting face, the Short-eared Owl will soon be one of your top ten birds.

A medium-sized owl, 38 cm long, with a wingspan of around 100 cm.

LOOK FOR A long-winged owl quartering the ground over the moors. For a sizeable bird, it can be difficult to spot, but equally the round, pale face with yellow eyes, and the mottled but rather striking plumage can stand out, especially when it perches on a fence post. In spring, its aerial display, accompanied by a rapid series of deep, hooting calls and loud wing-clapping, is exciting to watch even from a distance.

WHEN TO GO Present all year round, but scarce as a breeding bird; most sightings are in the winter, when numbers are boosted by birds from other parts of Europe.

This owl regularly flies during the day, but is especially active around dawn and dusk.

WHERE TO GO Open country, upland moorland and rough grassland, especially in the wilder parts of northern England and Scotland. In winter they tend to congregate on heathland, and grassland near the coast.

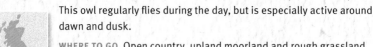

SCIENCE STUFF

THE NUMBER OF SHORT-EARED OWLS VARIES FROM YEAR TO YEAR AND IS CLOSELY LINKED TO THE AVAILABILITY OF ITS MAIN PREY, THE SHORT-TAILED FIELD VOLE. WHEN VOLES ARE SCARCE, THE OWLS LAY FEWER EGGS AND RAISE FEWER CHICKS, BUT IN GOOD YEARS MORE EGGS ARE LAID AND THEY MAY EVEN HAVE TWO BROODS.

The Great British · Wildlife Hunt

15

Red Grouse

A familiar bird of moorland, the Red Grouse is known for the comic way it pops up out of the heather. Numbers are high in areas managed for shooting – best that it keeps its head down!

Length 40 cm. The female (above) is similar to the male, but lacks red 'combs' over the eye.

LOOK FOR Red Grouse are often quite tame and allow a close approach, although the finely barred and mottled plumage provides beautiful camouflage. But, if surprised, they have a fast, whirring flight, low over the heather. They can also run fast and may be seen crossing paths or other open areas. The male's red combs are very obvious in spring when he displays to the female, fluffing out his feathers too. Males can be quite noisy in spring, making a series of cackling calls, which some say sound like *go-back, go-back.*

WHEN TO GO Resident in Britain all year round, it can be encountered at any time.

WHERE TO GO A bird of extensive Heather moorland, mostly in the uplands. Red Grouse breed amongst thick Heather and feed largely on young heather shoots, adding berries and seeds to their diet in the autumn.

NEWS EXTRA! Heather moors are managed for Red Grouse by burning strips of moorland in rotation. This results in a steady supply of nutritious young Heather shoots for the grouse to eat, as well as taller, older Heather for nesting and shelter. The chicks are fed on invertebrates.

Dartford Warbler

A small bird with plenty of character; searching for Dartford Warblers will enliven a heathland walk at any time of year.

Length 12.5 cm. Both males and females are a striking but subtle mixture of dark wine-red and slate-grey, although the females are a little duller.

LOOK FOR A small bird that gives the impression of an over-large head due to its tendency to puff out its throat and raise its crest. It usually skulks low down, so look for movements amongst the bushes or spot a dark, long-tailed bird flying low from one clump of Heather or gorse to another. If you are lucky you may find one perched on top of a gorse bush, singing, or perhaps giving you an inquisitive glance as you pass by.

WHEN TO GO Present all year round, but most active in spring when singing and displaying. Numbers can fall after cold winters when heavy snow prevents the birds from feeding.

WHERE TO GO Only found in the south and east of Britain, almost exclusively on heathland with plenty of tall gorse and other bushes, especially near the coast. Dartford Warblers rarely move far from their territories and are be found in the same locations year after year.

TOP TIP ★ Dartford Warblers are found in a similar habitat to Stonechats, on heaths and coastal areas of southern England, (see page 66), so where you find one, look for the other.

The Great British Wildlife Hunt

15

Adder

Britain's only poisonous snakes, Adders should never be handled. They are usually shy, however, and you will have to outwit an Adder to see it well.

LOOK FOR Sheltered, dry, south-facing ground at the edges of bushes and tangles, which is warmed by the sun. Adders can be well camouflaged, so look carefully for them tucked in under the heather and gorse as they bask. Walk softly and quietly too, as they will slip off into cover if they feel the vibration of your feet.

Adders can be up to 65 cm long. Males are greyish, while females are larger and browner. Both sexes have a distinctive black zig-zag along the back.

WHEN TO GO Adders are active from February to October, hibernating underground in the winter. A warm day between late February and early April is the best time to look for them, as they have just emerged from hibernation and spend long periods basking – only rain or cold winds will put them off.

WHERE TO GO Moorland, heathland and open woodland that was once heathland. Adders can also be found in the wetter, boggier areas of moorland and heathland, hunting for frogs and small rodents.

NEWS EXTRA! You will be very lucky to see this many Adders in one place, but they will often choose the same basking site having emerged from the same 'hibernaculum'. The ground temperature at these basking sites can often be 10°C higher than the air temperature.

40 The Great British Wildlife Hunt

Emperor Moth

A stunning, day-flying moth with a very conspicuous caterpillar and cocoon. Indeed, it is so obvious that its ability to deter predators is clearly working very well.

The female's wingspan can be 8cm, males are smaller.

LOOK FOR The adult moth is unmistakable, with some of the best 'warning' colouration of any British insect – the eyespots on the wings act to startle would-be predators. On the wing, however, the Emperor can be mistaken for a butterfly as it flies fast and erratically over the heather, rarely perching.

WHEN TO GO Adults fly from April to June, sometimes later in the north. They emerge from the cocoons early in the day and this is the best time to find them as they sit on the vegetation, drying off their wings. The larvae feed in the open and can be found from May to August.

WHERE TO GO Heathland and moorland on sunny days in spring – indeed anywhere where the larval food plants grow. Eggs are mostly laid on heather, but also on brambles, alder buckthorn, willows and hawthorns.

Mature caterpillar.

Immature caterpillars.

Cocoon.

TOP TIP ★ Look for the fibrous, flask-shaped cocoons attached to plant stems, mainly heather and gorse. These can be more noticeable in the winter, but don't take them away – they may be occupied by a pupa.

The Great British Wildlife Hunt
10

Heath Milkwort

Trailing over other vegetation with its clusters of sparkling flowers, this plant is only found on acid soils, often in the company of many other interesting plants and animals.

Heath Milkwort, with blue flowers.

The leaves at the base of the stem are opposite pairs, but are often buried in the surrounding vegetation.

LOOK FOR Milkworts are found close to the ground, scrambling through other vegetation. Amongst the yellow flowers of gorse in spring or the purple of the heathers in August, their small, jewel-like, purple, blue, pink or white flowers attract attention – such a variety of flower colours in a single species is rare in a wild flower. Look more closely and you can see the flower's fingered 'lip'.

WHEN TO GO The flowering period is long, extending from April to early September.

WHERE TO GO Heaths, moors and grassland on acid soils. Milkworts will grow amongst other plants on both dry and wet parts of the heath.

TOP TIP ✷ Common Milkwort is very slightly larger, with the leaves at the base of the stem arranged alternately; otherwise it has similar flowers, with a similar range of colours. It is found in grassland on chalk and limestone.

Tree Pipit

The Tree Pipit's song and its aerial song-flight are among the iconic sights and sounds of heath and moorland, evoking an incredible sense of place.

Males and females are similar.

Length 15cm. Pipits are small, slender, streaky birds with a fine bill; altogether smaller and slimmer than a Skylark.

LOOK FOR Look for a Tree Pipit perched in a tree, from which it will launch itself into the air, singing as it rises and then 'parachuting' back down to the tree with its legs dangling in a characteristic pose. The song is an unmistakable series of trills and sweet *seoo seoo seoo* notes. When not singing. Tree Pipits feed on the ground, usually near or under cover, and are then hard to see until they are disturbed, when they often fly up and sit in a tree.

WHEN TO GO They are summer visitors, arriving in April and May and leaving again for Africa in August and September. It can be rather difficult to find after the breeding season, and May and June are the best months to see them.

WHERE TO GO Heathland and moorland with scattered trees, also the edge of nearby woodland and recently cleared or young conifer plantations.

TOP TIP ★ Tree Pipits are difficult to distinguish from the much commoner Meadow Pipits – habitat and song are the best features. Meadow Pipits prefer rough, open, grassland and moorland and rarely sing from tall trees; their song flight often starts and ends on the ground.

TREE PIPIT SINGING

The Great British Wildlife Hunt
15

Green Tiger Beetle

It is often the first week of May before heathland starts to come alive after the winter and this is the best time to see this magnificent ground beetle in action.

Up to 14 mm long.

LOOK FOR An iridescent green beetle, especially brilliant in the sunshine, with obvious yellow spots – it is the only large beetle you will see with this colour pattern. Green Tiger Beetles have long legs and run fast along the ground; they are rarely seen on vegetation. When disturbed they will rise up to effortlessly fly past your ear with a faint buzzing.

WHEN TO GO Adults are active from April to September, but may be most numerous in May or June. Choose a sunny day and they will be on the move.

WHERE TO GO Open areas on heathland and in the sunny rides of surrounding woods – look especially for patches of sandy, bare ground with sparse vegetation. Green Tiger Beetles are often seen hunting on tracks and footpaths and can be fairly numerous.

TOP TIP ★ Green Tiger Beetles are ferocious predators. Watch them stalking their prey, which includes any small invertebrates, such as spiders, caterpillars and ants –and check out those huge jaws.

The Great British Wildlife Hunt

25

Common Lizard

This small reptile is so easily overlooked that most of us do not register its presence, but look in the right place amongst the heather and you may be lucky enough to spot one.

Long toes

15cm from nose to tail. The overall colour can vary from brown to green.

LOOK FOR Lizards can move very fast and most sightings are a glimpse of a disappearing tail – they usually have a favourite burrow close by into which they vanish. However they do like to bask, so look for sunny spots in or on heather bushes and on bare ground; on overcast days they may slow down and can be seen and even photographed sitting out in the open.

WHEN TO GO Active from March to November. In winter they hibernate below ground. Go in the early morning or late in the day to catch them basking.

WHERE TO GO Heathland, moorland and rough grassy areas close by. Catch them basking on isolated rocks, stones, grassy tussocks or fallen trees. Lizards also use the nooks and crannies found in rocky outcrops and stone or brick walls for shelter, and these can be great places to look for them.

Typical habitat.

Smooth Newt

TOP TIP ★ Lizards and newts can be told apart by their skin. Lizards are reptiles and have scaly skin. Newts are amphibians with skin that is smooth and velvety.

The Great British Wildlife Hunt

40

Nightjar

A summer walk at dusk is the only way to see Nightjars as they are nocturnal birds. You will then find out why heaths and moors were often thought to be haunted!

LOOK FOR A long-winged and long-tailed mottled brown bird. You will probably only see it silhouetted against the sky, but if one flies close by, the white spots on the male's wings can be seen. A Nightjar could be mistaken for a Kestrel, which can be active surprisingly late in the evening. Nightjars never hover; rather they fly with a mixture of silent flapping and long, low glides.

Length 27 cm. The shape in flight is rather like a Kestrel, but a Nightjar is a little smaller.

WHEN TO GO Nightjars are summer visitors, arriving in early May and leaving in late July. Beautifully camouflaged, they sit, unseen, on the ground during the day. This is a bird of the night, so look for it at dusk; just when you think it is beginning to get too dark – that is the time to watch their fantastic flight and listen for their calls.

WHERE TO GO Heathland and moorland, also woodland clearings and 'clear-felled' areas in conifer plantations.

TOP TIP ✳ The first sign of a Nightjar is usually the unmistakable churring call, often given from a hidden perch in a tree. As dusk falls they fly haphazardly around, catching moths on the wing: fantastic!

Heath Spotted Orchid

A flamboyant but delicate flower that stands out beautifully amongst the rather drab surroundings of heather and grass on a midsummer moor.

10-25 cm tall.

The petals usually have many faint dots and dashes on the lip.

LOOK FOR A slender upright plant with spotted leaves. The wide, pale pink or near-white flowers stand out like no other amongst the Heather and sedges in its favourite moorland habitats. The lower petal of the flower (the 'lip') is very broad and often covered in fine pink dots – it can resemble a very full, pleated skirt.

WHEN TO GO Flowers mid-May to July, earlier in drier habitats and later in wetter ones and in the far north.

WHERE TO GO Heaths and moors, especially in the damper areas around peat bogs and wet flushes where Cross-leaved Heath, with its grey-green leaves and dusty-pink flowers, also grows. There may be many hundreds of orchids in one area and their presence usually indicates a good area for plants generally. Damp, unimproved meadows and pastures in the hills can also hold colonies.

TOP TIP ★ The Common Spotted Orchid also has spotted leaves and may be found in similar places, but the lip of that flower is deeply divided into three equal lobes. Southern and Northern Marsh Orchids have unspotted leaves and darker, more purplish flowers.

Northern Marsh Orchid   *Common Spotted Orchid*

The Great British Wildlife Hunt

20

Golden-ringed Dragonfly

One of the largest and most spectacular British dragonflies, its large bright green eyes are mesmerising and add to the drama of any sighting.

LOOK FOR Both males and females have black bodies with yellow bands across the abdomen and cannot be mistaken for any other species. The Golden-ringed Dragonfly flies fast and is a fearsome predator, catching mostly flying midges. Males patrol a stretch of stream bank and defend it from other males. They always perch with wings outstretched and may rest up for some time to allow good views – if you can spot them.

WHEN TO GO Adults fly from the end of May until September, but July and August are the best months to find them. Like all dragonflies, the nymphs develop under water and when they are fully grown, crawl up onto plant stems in the morning to allow the adult form to emerge.

WHERE TO GO Common on moorland with shallow, acid streams in upland areas, and also found on some lowland heaths. Adults can be found patrolling patches of heather and scrub away from water and in the rides of surrounding woodland.

TOP TIP ★ At 11cm long, the female is the largest British dragonfly. The long ovipositor at the tip of the abdomen is used to lay eggs into shallow, gravelly streambeds, so look for them along small streams. Egg-laying takes place in the morning.

Round-leaved Sundew

Glistening red jewels of the bog – cast your eyes to the ground to see the sundew's spectacular mechanism for catching prey – it is one of the few British insectivorous plants.

LOOK FOR Roughly circular leaves, the size of a five-pence piece, with long reddish hairs, each tipped with a jewel-like droplet of clear liquid. These are not water, but a sticky fluid secreted by the plant to trap unwary insects. Sundews often occur in dense groups in bare muddy patches or on tussocks of sphagnum mosses.

Leaves up to 1 cm across. Some leaves may be curled up – these may have an insect inside them.

WHEN TO GO The distinctive leaves are visible from April to October, while the white flowers, which open one at a time on slender stems up to 15cm long, appear from June to August.

WHERE TO GO True bog plants, sundews only occur in open, wet places around pools, tiny streams and flushes on the acid soils of moors and heaths. The bare ground along boggy paths is a good place to look.

SCIENCE STUFF

ONCE THE LEAVES HAVE TRAPPED AN INSECT, OTHER LIQUIDS ARE SECRETED THAT DIGEST THE INSECT'S BODY; THE LEAF THEN ABSORBS THE RESULTANT NUTRITIOUS SOUP. THIS EXTRA FOOD ALLOWS SUNDEWS TO THRIVE IN AN OTHERWISE INHOSPITABLE ENVIRONMENT.

The Great British Wildlife Hunt

25

Minotaur Beetle

This beetle – the male with its three horns – means business! It uses the horns in battle, just like the mythical Greek monster, half-man, half-bull, that it is named after.

Female.

Male 15mm long and unmistakable.

LOOK FOR Both males and females may be seen steadily walking over the ground rolling balls of Rabbit dung or digging burrows in which to bury their prizes, on which the female will then lay eggs, the dung providing food for the larvae. The burrows are characteristic, about the diameter of a little finger, either covered in triangular mounds of loose earth, or sealed up. You may see lots in a small area.

Minotaur burrow.

WHEN TO GO Although mostly nocturnal, adults can be seen on dull, mild days from March to June and again from September to November when fresh adults emerge from the burrows.

WHERE TO GO Sandy grassland and heathland with obvious signs of Rabbit activity. Look in areas of sparse vegetation, close to Rabbit scrapes, sometimes on paths and path edges.

Female rolling dung

NEWS EXTRA! Minotaur Beetles will surprise you if you pick them up as they make a disgruntled noise – a cross between a squeak and a sneeze.

Silver-studded Blue

A captivating butterfly, the combination of its colonial lifestyle and sedentary habits mean you can sit and watch a whole colony.

The silver 'studs' are the small spots in the centre of the black circles on the hindwing, and can be hard to see – try using binoculars.

Male.

Female – note orange spots.

LOOK FOR Silver-studded Blues live in well-defined colonies that can be spectacular, the butterflies never straying far from each other. They are the only blue butterflies to be seen in large numbers on Heathland. Males fly over heather and gorse searching for females and it is common to see them mating.

WHEN TO GO Adults fly from the middle of June to late August. They roost together in heather, moving out in the early morning; colonies are active all day, even in overcast weather.

WHERE TO GO Heathland in southern Britain, also very locally on chalk grassland and sand dunes. Find sheltered, south-facing areas of short vegetation with lots of bare ground. Adults rarely feed but may be seen on Bell Heather. The eggs are laid close to the ground and the caterpillars feed mainly on heathers (in chalky areas they use Bird's-foot Trefoil).

SCIENCE STUFF

CATERPILLARS ARE RARELY SEEN. THEY ARE USUALLY SURROUNDED BY BLACK ANTS, FOR WHICH THE LARVAE SECRETE A SUGARY LIQUID. IT IS THOUGHT THE ANTS MAY PROTECT THE LARVAE FROM PREDATORS, EVEN TAKING THEM INTO THEIR UNDERGROUND NESTS TO PUPATE.

The Great British Wildlife Hunt

25

Cranberry

Take a close look at this tiny plant – the flowers are an exquisite mix of pink and purple. British Cranberries were once collected and eaten, but modern cranberry sauce comes from a rather larger American species.

LOOK FOR A tiny, trailing plant, with strings of leaves creeping over and through the surrounding vegetation. The small, oval, dark green leaves are just 10mm long and the flowers, although tiny, are unusual and worth a close look – the four petals are pressed backwards to reveal a bundle of eight stamens (the male part of the flower) clustered around the single style (the female portion). The berries are red.

Flowers tiny, just 6-10 mm across.

WHEN TO GO Cranberry flowers from June to August and both flowers and young fruits can be seen on the plants in late summer.

WHERE TO GO The wettest parts of heaths and moors, often around bog pools, where it creeps amongst heathers and mounds of *Sphagnum* moss, often in the company of Round-leaved

Sundew (see p. ooo). Tread carefully amongst the many other special plants that also grow in these places, and be aware of deep, muddy hollows.

NEWS EXTRA! In former times Cranberry fruits were collected and used in local recipes, even though they are small and very tart. Due to drainage it has disappeared from much of the lowlands, but is still common in the uplands of the north and west of Britain.

The Great British Wildlife Hunt
30

Dodder

Resembling a mass of red cotton threads rather than a plant, this fascinating wild flower is a true parasite and one of the strangest things to be found on a heath.

LOOK FOR The red, leafless, thread-like stems are unique, making identification easy. The tiny pale pink flowers appear in pompom-like clusters along the stems.

Flower clusters only 10mm across.

WHEN TO GO Dodder begins to appear as red, cotton-like threads in mid-May. From July to September these tiny threads can reach plague proportions, completely covering the host and becoming very obvious. Dodder is an annual plant – all traces vanish by the winter.

WHERE TO GO Dodder is mostly parasitic on gorse and Heather, usually on the drier parts of a heath, and is particularly fond of the re-growth after gorse has been cut.

SCIENCE STUFF

RELATED TO BINDWEEDS, DODDER HAS NO ROOTS OF ITS OWN. GERMINATING ON THE GROUND, THE SEEDLING SENDS UP A TWINING SHOOT THAT SEEKS OUT A HOST AND ATTACHES ITSELF WITH TINY STICKY PADS. THESE PADS PRODUCE ORGANS THAT PENETRATE THE HOST'S TISSUE AND STEAL NUTRIENTS FROM IT.

The Great British Wildlife Hunt

25

Solitary wasps

A large group of insects, all of which are colourful, lively and absorbing to watch. Once you have spotted a few you will always be on the lookout for them.

RED-BANDED DIGGER WASP

Collects caterpillars to feed its larvae. Up to 25mm long.

SAND DIGGER WASP

Collects adult weevils to feed its larvae. 12mm long.

Solitary wasps, as their name suggests, make individual nests, usually in holes in sandy ground. But, although 'solitary', they can nest in large, scattered colonies when their nest holes become obvious.

LOOK FOR There are many species of solitary wasp in Britain, and a large number have these black-and-red or black-and-yellow colour combinations. Solitary wasps can be told from solitary bees by the lack of pollen-collecting hairs on their legs. Adult solitary wasps feed on flowers, but they feed their maggot-like larvae on other invertebrates. Watch for female wasps digging in the ground and carrying prey to the holes, and for male wasps searching for females.

WHEN TO GO Most species are active from May to September. Go at the warmest, sunniest times to see the most activity – generally from late morning to late afternoon.

WHERE TO GO Occur throughout Britain on heathland and areas close by with short grassland. Bare ground and warm, sunny spots on sandy, well-drained soils. Sandy banks can be good, but well-trodden paths are a real favourite.

TOP TIP ★ Sit quietly when you find a group of wasp holes. You should see all sorts of behaviour and come to recognise different wasps. Watch also for other parasitic insects investigating the nest holes or following the females in. Altogether fascinating.

Grayling

A large, flappy butterfly that wafts along on the breeze, only to disappear from view the moment it settles on the ground.

Male and females are similar, and about the size of a Meadow Brown. Sits on the ground, tilted towards the sun, but only rarely spreads its wings.

LOOK FOR Settled on the ground with its wings closed, the cryptic colouration of the Grayling makes it almost invisible, despite its relatively large size. It will fly up when disturbed and, after a short, undulating flight, pitch back down to the ground, making it hard to see. Females lay their eggs on grasses and are much harder to spot as they stay close to suitable grassy clumps.

WHEN TO GO Sunny days in late summer; adults are on the wing from July to mid-September. Graylings can be quite numerous, and the scattered colonies sometimes contain hundreds of individuals.

WHERE TO GO Graylings need dry, well-drained soils with sparse vegetation and sandy, stony or rocky ground. They are common on lowland heaths, especially near the coast and on any short grassland, including sand dunes. Look for them on bare ground, especially tracks and paths. Graylings will also drink from puddles and obtain nectar from heathers, thistles, Bird's-foot Trefoil, brambles and clovers.

TOP TIP ✳ Once you have located your Grayling, follow it quietly and enjoy its interactions with other Graylings and, in fact with every other insect that it sees.

WETLANDS

Water is everywhere. It falls from the sky, seeps up through the ground, forms streams, rivers, ponds and lakes and eventually returns to the sea, to be continually re-cycled. Water is essential for all life, including humans. We drink it, wash in it, cook with it, and use it for industry and for recreation. And, of all the habitats in Britain, wetlands include some of the most natural – think of an upland stream, tumbling down a rocky valley – but also some of the most artificial – canals, reservoirs, ditches and ponds – and some of the most intensively managed – rivers and streams that are straightened and deepened, even nature reserves where water levels are controlled by pumps and sluices. Whatever the origin, many plants and animals have had to overcome being permanently waterlogged in order to live there and have evolved into many varied and fascinating species just waiting to be discovered.

Rivers and streams

Many rivers originate in the uplands and although they vary hugely in character – especially in length: the River Severn is the longest river in Britain at 354km (220 miles) from source to sea, while the River Scavaig on the Isle of Skye is the shortest at just 400m. Rivers can be divided into three recognisable stages:

The upper reaches are where the river begins, usually in a valley with steep sides, such as a gorge, and often with waterfalls and pools. The water is cold, fast-flowing, and well aerated as it tumbles over the rocks. This is the home of Dippers (p.101), spawning Trout (p.120) and Golden-ringed Dragonflies (p.78) as well as the aquatic stages of many mayflies (p.110). Mosses and liverworts can be found on the damp rocks but most aquatic plants can only gain a hold in sheltered pools.

The middle reaches flow through a broader valley with some sort of floodplain on either side of the river. The water warms and the river slows as the gradients are not as steep. It starts to meander and, on the outside of the bends, low cliffs are cut by the faster flowing water. They are good places to look for Kingfishers (p.97) and sun-loving insects. In the inside of the bends the water flows more gently and silt is deposited on beaches and sandbars, allowing plants to grow.

The lower reaches are where the river is at its deepest and broadest, meandering across wide, fertile valleys (the valley sides may not be obvious) and often with a large floodplain. Some rivers flow through the countryside but often the lower reaches have been exploited by humans – many of our largest cities and towns have grown up beside a wide river. Once heavily polluted, the water quality in nearly all the UK's rivers is much improved, to the extent that some superb river wildlife can be found in the centre of many towns. When the river finally meets the sea it may pass through a great city or harbour and much of the silt is deposited in estuaries, often creating saltmarshes and mud banks (see p.125). Large rivers may not be the easiest habitats to explore but are usually good for general wildlife watching, especially if you can find a quiet spot. Use a good map and explore some of the smaller associated wetlands and don't forget to get up close.

River dipping

There is every reason to take a net and tray with you on visits to rivers and streams and spend time discovering some of the less obvious plants and animals. Shallow rivers and streams are fun to wade in – a real experience of river life. Look for streams with low grassy banks that allow safe, easy access, and for quiet fords (where a road crosses a small, shallow river).

With deeper rivers, find a low bridge with little or no traffic where you can sit and dangle a net. For river dipping a long-handled net with a flat, squared-off tip is best. Use the tip of the net to gently disturb the gravel, moving it carefully upstream. Any creatures hiding in the gravel will be dislodged and drift down into your net. Tip the contents of the net into a tray full of water (white is best) and look for dragonfly and mayfly nymphs and a host of other creatures.

Always be very cautious when near rivers. Take someone with you, do not lean out from steep banks (you could slip, or they may be undercut and collapse) and do not go near to river or streams in times of flood.

Streams

Merely small rivers, streams tend to be shallow and fast-flowing at the source, becoming slower and gentler as they trickle down and merge into bigger streams and rivers. They vary depending on the type of rock and the landscape that they are flowing through: upland streams often have very clear, shallow water, while some of the finest in the lowlands are chalk streams. Both are great places to observe aquatic life.

A chalk stream.

Lakes and ponds

Characterised by their still water, lakes and ponds vary tremendously depending on how they were formed and where they are in the country. In general, those in the lowlands tend to have water that has passed through farmland and is rich in plant nutrients. They often support luxuriant vegetation. Those in the uplands tend to be more sparsely vegetated as they are often fed by rivers and streams that originate in peat bogs or run over hard granites and are therefore much lower in plant nutrients. Wherever they are, lakes and ponds are great places to look for wildlife at any time of year, sheltering birds in winter, providing safe nest sites in spring, and full of plants and insects in summer.

Natural lakes and ponds

Natural lakes and ponds are rather rare in the lowlands. They may be formed in natural depressions or by subsidence (caused by coal and salt mines). Others are found in broad river valleys where a meandering river has formed ox-bow lakes. In undisturbed habitats such ponds and lakes would come and go, forming and slowly silting up in a completely natural way, but human intervention, such as dredging, seldom allows this to happen.

In the uplands natural lakes and ponds are much more widespread. High rainfall combined provides a plentiful supply of water and ice age glaciers have carved out deep, U-shaped valleys, allowing the formation of long, deep lakes with lots of marginal habitats. Upland lakes and pools have very specialised plants and animals, but are often almost deserted in winter, even by birds.

Pond dipping

Pond dipping is a great way to see wildlife and you will be surprised at how many different creatures there are. You need a long-handled net (the stronger the better, and a rounded net will not get caught up so easily) and trays or pots to put your finds in – large margarine and ice cream tubs work well. Dip from the edge and sweep your net in one direction in the water. Try to dip in different places: open water, the shallows, under trees and amongst vegetation. Do not forget to put your finds back into the pond when you have finished, and always take someone with you when pond dipping, just in case.

Many venues organise pond-dipping events and these are well worth attending. You will soon become confident enough to try out your own local ponds or perhaps an upland pool, where the wildlife may be quite different.

Man-made lakes and ponds

Most lakes and ponds in England and Wales were constructed by humans for a special purpose. They are often some of our best-loved landscape features. Here are just a few examples:

VILLAGE PONDS provided water for animals and people – villages often grew up around them. Large or small, the best ones have a good variety of marginal and aquatic plants.

DEW PONDS were built in limestone areas to catch the rain before it drained through the porous rock and disappeared. Their fluctuating levels attract specialised plants and animals.

MILL PONDS provide a steady and reliable supply of water to a water mill.

FLOODED MEDIEVAL PEAT DIGGINGS created the Norfolk Broads, a network of rivers and lakes, ditches and grazing marshes. A new National Park, access is improving all the time.

DUCK DECOYS with radiating networks of pipes were built to trap ducks in large numbers.

GREAT ESTATES built ponds and lakes purely for ornament, often as part of landscaped grounds. Once kept very formal, increasingly a good fringe of marginal plants makes for good insect hunting.

Many of these are now 'redundant' as technology has passed them by and are used for recreation in the form of fishing and boating. Some are managed for wildlife and bird watching and these are some of the easiest wetland sites to get to know – they may have wooden boardwalks to make access easy and may even have pond-dipping platforms. Traditional village ponds are often disappointing, however. They may have a lot of cute ducks, but the ducks' food, trampling and droppings usually means murky water and few invertebrates.

Village ponds can be found throughout Britain.

A dew pond is shallow with fluctuating water levels.

The Norfolk Broads have reed-fringed deep lakes and marshes

Lakes in ornamental gardens often develop a rich wildlife community.

Canals

All of the canals in Britain were built by hand, mostly in the period 1760–1800, in order to move heavy goods around the country. Now their use is purely recreational and whether you are on or off the water, they can be great places to get up close to watch wildlife, especially when boat traffic is light or non-existent. Look for common birds

like Moorhens (p.103) and hawker dragonflies on sunny days. You may well be able to see Yellow Water-lilies (p.107) without taking a boat.

Reservoirs

Most reservoirs were built to store drinking water, but some older reservoirs were designed to supply canals. Some have concrete banks and provide limited wildlife interest, although they may attract lots of wintering ducks. Others have more natural banks and are much better for plants and animals, especially as the water levels fall in summer. Reservoirs often have access via public footpaths and many have one or more bird watching hides, great in winter when a wide variety of birds find shelter on these inland lakes. Look for Grey Herons (p.106), Cormorants (p.105) and even the magical Otter (p.104).

Wet meadows, marshes, fens and bogs

A range of habitats produced by rivers periodically flooding the adjacent land or by springs and seepages saturating the ground, they are usually drier in summer and wetter in winter.

Wet meadows are dominated by grasses and wild flowers. They are cut for hay in midsummer, and may then be grazed for a couple of months by cattle or sheep. Sadly, this traditional land use is now rare, and wet meadows are seldom seen away from conservation areas.

'Marsh' is a general term for any type of wet ground, but is often used when the land is not farmed. The type of vegetation depends on the amount of water, its quality, and whether it is acid, creating a bog (see p.63) or alkaline, creating a fen. Some marshes are dominated by Common Reed and reedbeds are particularly good for birds.

Marshes can be difficult to explore, but many are now reserves and have networks of trails and boardwalks. They are at their best in spring and summer.

Lakenheath Fen is a wetland created from former carrot fields.

Ditches and dykes

Usually dug to drain marshy ground, which is then cultivated or grazed. Ditches in arable farmland tend to be steep-sided and choked with rank vegetation, but unpolluted, well-managed ditches in grazing marshes can be full of aquatic life and have a wonderful collection of aquatic and marginal plants.

New wetlands

Wetlands are some of our rarest habitats due to drainage, but the increase in incidents of flooding and the threat of sea level rise have led to new areas of wetland being created all over Britain. This has to be good news for all our wetland wildlife. Many have good public access and will soon become special places in the landscape.

The Great British Wildlife Hunt

35

Water Vole

Scoring high on cuteness, the Water Vole is holding on as a British native by the skin of its large teeth! All sightings should be relayed to a county recorder.

LOOK FOR A chunky, dark brown rodent that swims with its nose in the air and makes a distinct 'plop' when diving into the water. When you see one, sit quietly and enjoy it as it swims, gathers plant stems for nest building, or sits nibbling plants at the water's edge. Also look for tracks and signs, such as flattened 'runs' in the grass, chewed stems, piles of droppings and paw prints in the soft mud.

WHEN TO GO During the day at any time of year. July can be the best month when they are busy feeding young, but they spend much of the winter in their burrows. Water Voles are vulnerable to disturbance so watch from a distance.

WHERE TO GO Well-vegetated, slow moving rivers with earthy banks for their burrows, also ponds, lakes, and ditches and streams running through reedbeds and marshes, always in clean water.

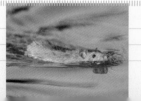

TOP TIP ✱ Brown Rats also live in waterside habitats, but the Water Vole has a rounded snout and a shorter, slightly furry tail (a rat's tail is long and naked).

The Great British Wildlife hunt

45

Bittern

You are more likely to see a Bittern now than at any time in the last 20 years. It is a conservation success story due to the creation and management of the reedbeds in which it nests.

Length 75cm, slightly smaller than a Grey Heron.

LOOK FOR Bitterns are very difficult to see when standing amidst the reeds. They have superbly camouflaged plumage and remain very still. In flight they are the only large, brown, heron-like birds with broad, rounded wings; they fly with their heads tucked in and legs trailing.

WHEN TO GO Mid summer, when the adults fly back and forth bringing food to the young. Also the winter months when they spread further afield and are best looked for when flying to roost in the evening. Bitterns rarely move away from cover but in hard frosts or snow they may become bolder and give watchers a brilliant view.

WHERE TO GO Wetlands and marshes with plenty of tall vegetation, especially reedbeds.

SCIENCE STUFF

THE BITTERN'S 'BOOM' SOUNDS LIKE THE DEEP NOISE PRODUCED WHEN YOU BLOW ACROSS THE NECK OF A BOTTLE. MALES WILL CALL DAY AND NIGHT IN SPRING AND EARLY SUMMER, AND IN STILL CONDITIONS THE BOOM CAN BE HEARD UP TO 5KM AWAY. FROM A LOW POINT OF 11 BOOMING MALES IN 1997, BITTERNS HAD INCREASED TO OVER 100 BOOMERS BY 2011.

The Great British Wildlife Hunt

25

Bearded Tit

The cheeky chappies of the reedbed: once you have found them, you could watch their amusing antics for hours, but, unfortunately, they usually move off quickly.

Male

Length 12.5cm. About the size of a Long-tailed Tit, but with a bigger body and shorter tail.

LOOK FOR Bearded Tits usually attract attention with their 'pinging' calls, which may be taken up by several birds. Look for movements in the reeds – perhaps a family group is feeding by catching flies and caterpillars – and for small flocks flying over the tops of the reeds. As the picture above shows, males do not have a 'beard'; it looks much more like a bold black moustache.

WHEN TO GO In calm weather, especially in the early morning and evening, they may shin up reeds and sit in full view. Bearded Tits are present all year round, usually breeding and wintering in the same reedbeds, and are particularly active in spring and summer when feeding young, and in autumn when they congregate in excitable flocks.

WHERE TO GO Large reedbeds, both inland and on the coast. In late autumn and winter they disperse and can turn up almost anywhere there are reedbeds, even small ones.

Female

NEWS EXTRA! An enigmatic species which occurs from Britain east to China. It is a puzzle because it is not related to the 'true' tits and has no close relatives in Europe.

The Great British Wildlife Hunt

25

Kingfisher

One of Britain's most colourful and glamorous birds, and one that never fails to produce a thrill of excitement with every encounter.

Length 15cm – the size of a House Sparrow but with a long bill.

LOOK FOR A unique, brightly coloured bird, but easily overlooked because of its small size and very fast flight. Kingfishers can be amazingly well camouflaged against the dappled light of overhanging trees or sparkling reflections on the water. Look for suitable perches on branches and tree stumps and listen for the sharp flight call.

WHEN TO GO Present all year round. Time your visits for periods when riverbanks are quiet or find stretches of river away from disturbance. In the spring, pairs can be very noisy and active.

WHERE TO GO Clean, slow-flowing rivers and streams, also lakes, reservoirs and canals with suitable banks for nesting.

TOP TIP ✳ The call, a loud, whistled zee or zee-tee is worth learning, as it will attract your attention as the bird flies fast along a river. It also calls when perched, particularly when a mate is nearby.

The Great British Wildlife Hunt

15

Marsh Harrier

From a handful of pairs in the 1970s to almost 400 pairs today, this majestic raptor floating over the reeds is now a more commonplace sight in many parts of England.

Male

Length 55cm, the size of a Common Buzzard, but with relatively long wings.

A spectacular food pass between a pair or an adult and juvenile is worth waiting for.

LOOK FOR A commotion amongst ducks, gulls and waders as they rise to mob a harrier. Marsh Harriers are highly visible when hunting, flying slowly over a marsh, periodically gliding with their wings held up in a characteristic V-shape, then dropping

down to grab prey with their long legs. In the breeding season watch for the fantastic food pass, in which the female flies up off the nest to catch food dropped by the male, flipping upside down as she does so.

WHEN TO GO Present all year. In the spring they can be particularly obvious when circling around high in the air, calling and displaying.

WHERE TO GO Reedbeds, marshes and farmland, often near the sea.

Female

TOP TIP ★ Males and females are different colours. The female has a straw-coloured cap and chocolate-brown wings; the male has grey wings with black tips and a grey tail.

Reed Bunting

Unlike many wetland songbirds, which can be incredibly hard to see, Reed Buntings perch in the open and attract attention with their bold markings.

Male

Length 15cm, the size of a House Sparrow.

Female

LOOK FOR A sparrow-sized bird. The male is distinctive with a black head, white moustache and white collar, and the habit of perching high on reeds or bushes to sing. The song is short and repetitive, a monotonous *chip-chip chew*. The female is streaky and rather like a female House Sparrow, but Reed Buntings often flit their tails, showing off their distinctive white outer tail feathers.

WHEN TO GO Present all year. Males are especially obvious when singing in spring and summer.

WHERE TO GO Wetland areas with plenty of tall vegetation: marshes, reedbeds, reed-filled ditches and bushy saltmarshes. In winter sometimes also found on stubble and in weedy fields, and may even visit gardens.

NEWS EXTRA! In winter sometimes forms flocks with a variety of other buntings and finches.

Water Scorpion

The Great British Wildlife Hunt
35

This is the holy grail of the pond dipper, a super-hero of a beast. To find one demonstrates considerable knowledge and skill.

23mm long, flattened and leaf-like.

LOOK FOR A supremely well-adapted water bug that cannot be mistaken for any other. If you watch carefully you may be able to spot one coming to the water's surface to collect air through the 12mm-long breathing tube on its rear end, or see one sitting on submerged vegetation. In general, however, you will need a pond net to find one. Water Scorpions are not strong swimmers and walk around rather than swim, stalking water beetles and small fish that they catch with their strong grasping forelegs. To catch one you will need to sweep it off its feet, so run the net along the bottom of a pond, especially amongst vegetation.

WHEN TO GO Active all year round.

WHERE TO GO Clean freshwater pools and lakes with plenty of water plants, also shallow, still backwaters in rivers and streams.

SCIENCE STUFF

THE TAIL HAS NO STING, BUT IS USED AS A SIPHON TO TAKE IN AIR, ALLOWING THE WATER SCORPION TO REMAIN SUBMERGED FOR UP TO 30 MINUTES.

Dipper

A characteristic and charming bird of fast-flowing streams and rivers in upland Britain, great to see on a riverside stroll particularly in the winter when many other birds have moved south.

Length 18cm, a little smaller than a Starling and with a rounded appearance.

LOOK FOR The only songbird in Britain that swims and even walks underwater looking for food. Out of the water it is a plump, Robin-shaped bird with a white bib and a short tail that is frequently cocked. Dippers perch on rocks in the water, bobbing up and down and occasionally diving into the water. They often fly fast and straight above the water, giving a penetrating sharp call: *stik*, *stik* as they go.

WHEN TO GO Resident in the uplands all year, Dippers rarely move far from their breeding areas.

WHERE TO GO Fast-flowing upland streams and rivers with plenty of rocks and boulders. Look especially around weirs and bridges; Dippers often choose to nest in holes and ledges under man-made structures.

SCIENCE STUFF

LIKE MANY OTHER BIRDS DIPPERS HAVE A TRANSPARENT 'THIRD' EYELID KNOWN AS A NICTITATING MEMBRANE. WHEN UNDERWATER IT HELPS TO KEEP THE EYES CLEAN AND FREE FROM GRIT. THE TRUE EYELID FLASHES CONSPICUOUSLY WHITE WHEN THE BIRD BLINKS.

The Great British Wildlife Hunt · **25**

The Great British Wildlife Hunt

35

Water Rail

You will need all your field skills to track down a Water Rail, as this attractive and interesting bird is a real challenge to see.

Length 26cm, considerably smaller than a Moorhen.

LOOK FOR A slim bird with a long red bill and black-and-white bars on the flanks. Usually difficult to spot, it spends most of the time in dense vegetation and you are more likely to hear its pig-like squeals. When one does appear, you may find yourself holding your breath in case you frighten it away, but relax – Water Rails can be quite confiding.

WHEN TO GO Resident all year. In autumn and winter British birds are joined by visitors from Europe and this is the time that you are most likely to spot a Water Rail, as the

vegetation has died down and they will wander further afield to find food.

WHERE TO GO Breeds in marshes and reedbeds. The best chance of seeing one is from a hide that overlooks a quiet, secluded place. If you are lucky you may see one skulking around at the base of the reeds or feeding on nearby mud or in shallow water.

SCIENCE STUFF

THE BODY OF THE WATER RAIL IS VERY NARROW – IN THE JARGON 'LATERALLY COMPRESSED' – TO ENABLE IT TO WALK THROUGH THE DENSELY PACKED REED AND SEDGE STEMS.

Moorhen

A common bird, the Moorhen is easy to identify and is not particularly shy, so you can follow the antics of their extended families from day to day.

Length 34cm.

LOOK FOR A blue-black bird with a white stripe along each flank and a red and yellow bill. Moorhens have large yellowish-green feet for padding around on wet mud and vegetation and flick their tails while walking and swimming, showing off the white undertail. They often occur in family groups; juveniles stay with the adults and may help feed the next brood, breaking off small pieces of water plant to feed to the tiny chicks. Newly hatched young are black and fluffy but with a red bald head and bulging eyes.

WHEN TO GO Resident all year round.

WHERE TO GO Freshwater lakes and ponds, rivers and streams, and farmland ditches; indeed, almost anywhere there is fresh water. In the winter small groups can be seen feeding on nearby farmland.

TOP TIP ★ Juveniles are brown, and lack the red and yellow bill and red forehead shield.

The Great British Wildlife Hunt

50

Otter

This once-rare mammal is making a welcome return to our waterways and can even be spotted in some of our largest towns and cities, reflecting improvements in river quality.

Up to 70cm long, the tail can be 40cm extra.

LOOK FOR These shy and generally nocturnal mammals are best seen by sitting and waiting if you hope to get anything more than a quick glimpse as a tail disappears maddeningly from view. In general, searching with binoculars from a waterside hide is a good idea, or you could use a car. It is easier to search for their tracks in soft mud: clear footprints will show five webbed toes. Look also for Otter poo, often left on a prominent log or tussock; it is dark, slimy, smells of fish and usually contains fish bones.

WHEN TO GO Resident all year, with dawn or dusk by far the best times to look. In coastal areas, go as the tide falls, when Otters may search rock pools for trapped fish.

WHERE TO GO Meandering rivers with plenty of vegetation and fallen trees, lakes that are well stocked with fish and, especially in northern Britain, sheltered coasts.

An Otter amongst the seaweed in Scotland.

TOP TIP ✴ A typical site for an Otter's holt, will have entrances both underwater and above ground.

The Great British Wildlife Hunt

10

Cormorant

With a pterodactyl-like profile as it dries its wings the Cormorant gives us an insight into the origin of birds – they are the direct descendants of dinosaurs.

80–100cm long – the size of a large goose.

LOOK FOR A long-bodied, lean black bird. It flies with its neck outstretched, looking just as prehistoric as when perched on a post or rock drying its wings. Cormorants dive for fish, disappearing completely under the water.

WHEN TO GO Present all year. Breeds in loose colonies on rocky cliffs and also, in a few places, on tall trees inland.

WHERE TO GO May be seen flying past or fishing in the sea almost anywhere, but most widespread in winter and more likely to be seen around rocky coasts in the breeding season. Commonly perches on groynes and breakwaters or on the beach. Especially during the winter frequents rivers, lakes, reservoirs and gravel pits.

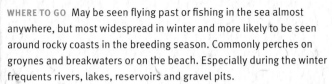

TOP TIP ✴ On northern and western coasts a Cormorant could be confused with a Shag, but that is smaller and slimmer, with a finer, darker bill and, in breeding plumage, a spiky crest. Shags are almost always found on rocky coasts and are very rare inland.

The Great British Wildlife Hunt

5

Grey Heron

The stately Grey Heron is a top predator, spending much of its time stalking stealthily through the water before swiftly stabbing at an unsuspecting fish.

Can be nearly one metre tall — it's a very large bird!

LOOK FOR Grey Herons are unmistakable. They often hunt and perch on their own, on the bank or in shallow water. They can remain motionless for some time, either with their heads held high, or hunched down, or leaning over, poised to catch a fish.

WHEN TO GO Present all year, Grey Herons breed in colonies, usually in tall trees and often well away from humans. These 'heronries' are used from year to year, and the birds can be seen squabbling and chasing each other from early February onwards.

WHERE TO GO Almost any wetland, both inland and on the coast: lakes and lagoons, slow-flowing rivers, marshes and estuaries and even small ponds.

TOP TIP ★ Herons sometimes visit garden ponds preying on (very obvious) goldfish, so watch for them flying over the rooftops.

Smooth Newt

Newts look a little primeval, especially the males in spring. They are not as fast as lizards and are more accommodating, allowing a view into their private lives.

The Great British Wildlife Hunt
20

Up to 11cm long. While on land their skin becomes drier and more leathery.

LOOK FOR In spring the males can look splendid with a fiery yellow-orange belly and throat, large black spots, and a magnificent crest running down the back. Females are smaller and have none of this finery. Do some pond dipping to see them up-close.

WHEN TO GO From February onwards newts will have returned to their ponds, laying eggs in April or May. Take a torch at night and shine it into the water for some of the best views; they can be very obvious in spring as the males chase the females around.

WHERE TO GO Freshwater ponds, ditches and canals with still, clean water, plenty of aquatic vegetation and shallow margins. Find a safe spot on the bank from which you can look into the water. After July most newts will leave ponds until the following year for a life on dry land, hiding under stones, in earth banks and even in walls.

NEWS EXTRA! There are two other species of newts in the UK: Great Crested Newt, which can be up to 18cm long and has warty skin, and Palmate Newt, which has an unspotted throat, webbed hind feet and a long, needle-like point at the tip of the tail. Both of these are common in some parts of Britain although the Great Crested Newt is a fully protected species in the UK.

The spring male has a bright, boldly spotted belly.

The Great British Wildlife Hunt

10

Marsh Marigold

These handsome, even regal, flowers are sometimes known as 'Kingcups'. They illuminate the drab greys and browns of an early spring marsh or river bank.

LOOK FOR Bright yellow flowers glowing like beacons in the shade of a wet woodland, drawing you to them. In the early spring the flowers of Marsh Marigold are an important source of pollen and nectar for insects. The large clumps of thick, kidney-shaped leaves are a glossy dark green and the stems are hollow; Marsh Marigold is altogether a much bigger version of a buttercup. This much-loved plant, once rather commoner than it is today, accumulated a number of local names: Kingcup is often used, but how about 'May blobs'!

WHEN TO GO Flowers from March to June, sometimes later.

WHERE TO GO The banks of stream, river and ditches, old, wet meadows and wet woodland.

TOP TIP ✳ Marsh Marigold may grow in very boggy ground so be sure to test the conditions underfoot before going up close.

The Great British Wildlife Hunt

25

Grass Snake

The Grass Snake may play dead when suddenly disturbed but keep watching and this harmless snake will 'wake up' and move off as if nothing had happened.

The largest British snake, it can grow to 150cm long.

LOOK FOR The yellow, white or cream-coloured band behind the head and more delicate body markings which separate this species from the Adder (p.70). Grass Snakes are well camouflaged and difficult to see when moving through long vegetation. Look for them basking in the sun to warm up, especially around heaps of vegetation in sheltered spots that catch the morning sun. Grass Snakes will hiss loudly if cornered and are best left undisturbed, but rarely strike out or bite.

WHEN TO GO On warm days in April they will be waking from hibernation and large numbers may be seen basking together in favourite spots. The eggs hatch in August or September and Grass Snakes may also be seen in groups at this time.

WHERE TO GO Rivers, canals, lakes, fens, ponds and their surrounding wet grassland. Grass Snakes will even venture into gardens with suitable habitat.

NEWS EXTRA! Grass snakes swimming make an unusual but delightful sight. You will be lucky to see this but patience often pays off.

Mayfly

The Great British · Wildlife Hunt · **10**

Adult mayflies have a short life, often just a single day, but the sight of males swarming over rivers and streams on a summer evening is a most beautiful spectacle.

Adult

Mayflies hatching from the water surface.

There are more than 50 species of mayflies in Britain. Spend time by a river, stream or ponds to watch the adults fly, and take a net to dip for the aquatic nymphs.

LOOK FOR Use binoculars to watch the sub-adult mayflies emerging from the water, peeling themselves away from the surface tension; sometimes hundreds 'hatch' at the same time. Then watch adult males dancing in swarms over the water to attract the females, and look for females dipping their abdomens into the water's surface as they lay their eggs.

The aquatic nymphs occur in different forms, but all have three pairs of legs, three tails and external gills, moving visibly along the sides of the body.

Swimming nymph.

Stone-clinging nymph.

Burrowing nymph.

WHEN TO GO Nymphs are found from early spring to late autumn, the adults from April to October. They are not strong fliers and only swarm on calm days.

WHERE TO GO Freshwater of all kinds: fast or slow moving rivers, or still water in lakes, ponds and ditches. Mayflies are very sensitive to pollution and you will only find the nymphs in clean water.

Sedge Warbler

Common in wetland habitats, where its rattling, but somehow cheerful, song is one of the characteristic sounds of spring.

13cm long, a little smaller than a sparrow and much slimmer.

LOOK FOR A small warbler, streaky brown above and creamy white below with a prominent white stripe above the eye, a good distinction from the otherwise similar Reed Warbler, which is found in some of the same habitats. Sedge Warblers move around amongst plant stems, often hidden from view – watch for the telltale movement of the reeds. They are more obvious when singing, and will occasionally launch into the air as if they suddenly forget themselves.

WHEN TO GO A summer visitor, arriving from Africa in late April and leaving in August. Often sings late into the evening.

WHERE TO GO Marshes and thick, tall vegetation beside lakes, rivers and ditches with plenty of meadowsweet, willowherbs, nettles, brambles and reeds.

TOP TIP ✳ The song is a loud jumble of harsh scratchy notes with the occasional sweet melodic whistles, often given from a perch on top of a bush or thicket, or in a short song flight.

The Great British • Wildlife Hunt
15

Pond Skater

Move in close to watch these predators at work. They use the surface film of the water to their advantage, scooping up less able insects for their meals.

Slender insects, up to 15mm long.

LOOK FOR Adults move fast across the water's surface. Like all insects they have six legs, but only four of the Pond Skater's are used to walk. The two front legs are adapted for catching prey and are kept tucked up until needed. Then, alerted by the struggles of any terrestrial insect that falls onto the water and is trapped in the surface film, the Pond Skater runs, glides and hops easily over the surface to grab its prey.

WHEN TO GO Sunny days from April to September. They hide on land in winter, but are often the first aquatic insects to appear in spring.

WHERE TO GO Ponds, lakes and ditches, and canals and rivers with areas of still water and emergent water plants, where the water is clean.

NEWS EXTRA! Nymphs (the young stages) have long legs but an odd shortened body. Look also for the Water Measurer, a relative of the Pond Skater but with quite different movements – a slow, jerking walk amongst emergent vegetation. The Water Cricket is another bug of the surface film, although not as widespread.

POND SKATER NYMPH

WATER MEASURER

WATER CRICKET

Marsh orchids

A very variable group of orchids, often found in large numbers and happily crossing with other species of wild orchid to produce some stunning flower spikes.

LOOK FOR Bearing dense spikes of pinkish-purple flowers, the plants grow individually, in loose groups or crowded together in large colonies, when they can produce some of the most spectacular floral displays in Britain. In the south look for Southern Marsh Orchid, which often has relatively pale flowers, while in the north the Northern Marsh Orchid has darker, more purplish flowers. Marsh orchids are often difficult to identify, however, complicated by the fact that they often cross with the spotted orchids to produce a range of hybrids – best to forget about names and just enjoy the spectacle.

WHEN TO GO Flowers from late May to July or early August.

WHERE TO GO Damp, flowery places, such as meadows, wet pastures, marshes, dune slacks, marshy gravel pits and sometimes road verges on damp soils.

SCIENCE STUFF

QUICK TO COLONISE NEW PLACES, SOME OF THE MOST SPECTACULAR DISPLAYS HAVE BEEN ON OLD INDUSTRIAL SITES, ESPECIALLY SODA AND FLY-ASH TIPS, AND IN CHALK OR LIMESTONE QUARRIES.

The Great British Wildlife Hunt
10

Whirligig Beetle

A group of small insects that hunt on the water's surface. The constant circling of a mass of Whirligigs on a pond can be mesmerising.

Around 10mm long

LOOK FOR Shiny black beetles on the water's surface are buoyed up by the surface tension. When the sun is out they zoom around like jet skis in a circle or figure of eight. If disturbed, the whole lot will disappear beneath the surface, but if you stand still you will see them bounce up again and continue their circling. When pond dipping, keep an eye out for the larvae. They look nothing like a beetle; they are long-bodied with many feathery appendages, allowing them to swim fast at the bottom of the pond.

WHEN TO GO Sunny days from early May to September. They spend the winter at the bottom of the pond.

WHERE TO GO Whirligigs require still water with plenty of aquatic vegetation. Find them on ponds, lakes, ditches and the still backwaters of rivers.

SCIENCE STUFF

BOTH ADULTS AND LARVAE ARE PREDATORY AND EAT MANY YOUNG MOSQUITOS. THE WHIRLIGIG'S EYES ARE IN TWO PARTS, HALF FOR SEEING ON THE SURFACE AND HALF FOR SEEING UNDERWATER – HOW CLEVER IS THAT? THIS MEANS THAT THEY CAN SEE YOU APPROACHING AND ARE NOT AS EASY TO CATCH IN A POND NET AS YOU MIGHT THINK!

Demoiselles

Who wouldn't love these dainty damselflies and want to watch them all day. It is easy to imagine how tales of fairies originated from these beautiful creatures.

BANDED DEMOISELLE

Male

BEAUTIFUL DEMOISELLE

Male

Female

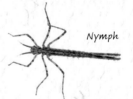

Nymph

There are two species in Britain, the Banded and the Beautiful Demoiselle.

LOOK FOR Large damselflies with a drifting, flappy flight over water; bursts of activity accompanied by periods perched on the marginal vegetation. Groups of both sexes together make a memorable sight. Males of both species have splendid metallic, blue-green bodies and richly coloured wings, uniformly dark in Beautiful Demoiselle but with a clear-cut dark band in the Banded Demoiselle.

WHEN TO GO From mid-May to September on warm, sunny days.

WHERE TO GO Beautiful Demoiselles prefer clean, fast-flowing streams and rivers with gravelly bottoms. Banded Demoiselles occur on slower-moving, muddier streams and rivers, canals and even lakes where there is plenty of bankside vegetation.

NEWS EXTRA! When the sun reaches the water at mid-day the males compete with each other in fantastic displays of agility.

The Great British Wildlife Hunt

30

Swallowtail

Our largest and most stunning butterfly, you will have to visit the Norfolk Broads to see it, but that's no great hardship and definitely worth trying to make the trip.

LOOK FOR A large butterfly flying fast over the tops of the vegetation or across rivers and dykes. The caterpillar is stunning too, at first black with a white band, mimicking a bird dropping, it then moults to become bright green with black and orange markings.

WHEN TO GO Adults are on the wing from late May to early July. In good years there may be a second generation in August. Calm, sunny weather is best. Caterpillars can be found from late June to the end of August.

WHERE TO GO The larval food plant is Milk Parsley, which in Britain is almost restricted to the Norfolk Broads. Access to the Broads is not always easy without a boat,

but there are some very good nature reserves with boardwalks extending into the marshes, and there is often also good access to riverbanks with tall vegetation. With luck, you can get great views of both adults and caterpillars.

TOP TIP ★ The Swallowtail is a fast flying butterfly and many sightings can be frustratingly brief. Red Campion, Ragged Robin and especially Marsh Thistle are favourite flowers, and it is worth 'staking out' any large patch of these.

Yellow Water-lily

With their huge rounded leaves and stalked, neon-yellow flowers, these lilies give a sense of theatre to large ponds and lakes.

The leaves can be 40cm across.

LOOK FOR Yellow flowers and large leaves, each about the size of a dinner plate. Indeed, 'dinner plate and the brandy glass' is an aptly descriptive name (although the common name for the flowers is 'brandy bottle', they look more like a glass). The flowers give off a faint smell of alcohol, attracting the small flies that pollinate them.

WHEN TO GO The floating leaves are visible from April or May and the flowers from June to September. The seedheads are visible in autumn but the leaves break up and the plants soon disappear below the water.

WHERE TO GO Lakes, canals, ditches, ponds and slow-flowing rivers, especially sheltered backwaters. Generally in clean, deep water.

TOP TIP ★ A difficult plant to get close to unless you are in a boat or canoe, due to its preference for open water. If you are in a boat, don't lean over the side to sniff the flowers!

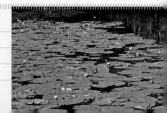

The Great British Wildlife Hunt
25

Marsh Helleborine

One of Britain's most glamorous orchids and perfection in miniature; move in close to appreciate the delicate colours and fine frills of the flowers.

Up to 30cm tall, with as many as 25 flowers on each spike.

LOOK FOR Spikes of pale flowers that stand out amongst the darker vegetation. The colour of the flower varies; from near white to pale pink or even beetroot-red. Marsh Helleborine rarely occurs singly and in certain special places can be found by the thousand, with no space to tread between them.

WHEN TO GO In flower from late June to early August.

WHERE TO GO Wet, marshy ground on poor soils, with short vegetation (usually below knee-height) and some bare areas – the plants are often found beside paths. Fens, marshes and dune-slacks are ideal habitats, especially where the ground water is chalky.

TOP TIP ∗ Recognising suitable habitat is the key to finding Marsh Helleborines; they are often hidden between the tussocks of Black Bog-rush, a tall, rather dull grey sedge.

Flower-rich fen.

Damp dune-slacks.

Black Bog-rush.

The Great British Wildlife Hunt

15

Southern Hawker

Even if you have not noticed a Southern Hawker, it has noticed you and will usually come and find you, hovering at close range to take a good look.

Males have a bright green thorax and some blue on the abdomen.

Females are greenish-yellow with obvious black stripes.

LOOK FOR Brightly coloured males patrolling their territories, flying up and down looking for females and catching small insects. A single male may keep a small pond to itself, or share a canal bank with several other males, each one spaced about 50m apart. Females visit these territories and, after mating (which often takes place away from the water), she returns to lay eggs in any soft woody material at the water's edge. Listen for the loud rustle of wings as she manoeuvres into position amongst the vegetation.

WHEN TO GO On the wing from late June to the end of September, they will even fly on quite dull days. When ready to emerge, the aquatic nymphs clamber up stout plant stems and the adults hatch.

WHERE TO GO Breeds in ponds of all sizes, including garden ponds, lakes and canals; also often seen in sheltered woodland rides.

SCIENCE STUFF
THE NYMPH OF THE SOUTHERN HAWKER SPENDS UP TO THREE YEARS LIVING UNDERWATER. A GREAT PREDATOR, IT STALKS AND EATS ANYTHING IT CAN CATCH, EVEN TADPOLES AND SMALL FISH.

The Great British Wildlife Hunt 20

Brown Trout

Looking down from a bridge into a shallow stream and watching the Brown Trout jostling for position beneath you is one of the pleasures of summer.

Adults can be 50cm or more long, but are usually smaller, around 25cm.

LOOK FOR A beautiful fish with a covering of dark reddish spots, each surrounded by a pale border. The background colour can vary depending on the surroundings, from bright silver in lakes to very dark in muddy pools, but the spots are characteristic. Only three months after they hatch the young trout ('fry') are miniature replicas of the adults, although only about 1.5cm long. Immature fish have blue-grey spots.

WHEN TO GO A warm summer's day, with a little cloud overhead (to help your view of the river) is by far the best time to watch trout taking flies from the water's surface or moving dreamily, close to the bottom of the stream. Male and female Brown Trout can be seen together when they are spawning from January to March.

WHERE TO GO Clean, well-oxygenated, freshwater streams, rivers and lakes. The young (fry) hatch in fast-flowing streams and need small pools in which to shelter.

RAINBOW TROUT, A NORTH AMERICAN SPECIES, IS COMMONLY INTRODUCED TO RIVERS. IT HAS FINE SPOTTING AND AN OBVIOUS PURPLE BAND ALONG ITS SIDE.

NEWS EXTRA! Confusingly, 'Sea Trout' is the same species as 'Brown Trout' – merely a different form. It is not known why some trout leave the rivers and head seawards in a similar manner to Salmon. They usually just lurk around the coast, however, before returning to the rivers to breed.

The Great British Wildlife Hunt

10

Purple Loosestrife

A striking plant, familiar beside ponds, lakes and streams, take a long, careful look at their spires of delicate, colourful flowers.

LOOK FOR Tall, upright, sturdy plants with several spikes of purple flowers. Look closely at the petals, which appear to be delicately crumpled. When growing in the sun, the flowers of Purple Loosestrife are great favourites with bees, butterflies and many other insects and all this activity may also attract your attention.

Can be very tall – up to 120cm.

WHEN TO GO Flowers from June to August or September.

WHERE TO GO Damp meadows, marshes, the margins of ponds, lakes and ditches, and even damp woodland rides.

SCIENCE STUFF

THE FLOWERS PRODUCE COPIOUS NECTAR TO ATTRACT POLLINATING INSECTS, WHICH MOVE RAPIDLY FROM ONE PLANT TO ANOTHER. LATER THE STEMS CAN BEND OVER WITH THE WEIGHT OF SEED PRODUCED.

The Great British Wildlife Hunt

15

Frogbit

This dainty and attractive water plant has a 'now you see me now you don't' kind of existence. You need to be around at just the right time of the year to enjoy the flowers.

Leaves only 3cm across.

LOOK FOR Small, round leaves, similar to a miniature water-lily. The attractive flowers grow on a short stalk and have three white petals surrounding the central yellow stamens. The plants are not attached by roots to the bottom mud and float freely on the water's surface, spreading via floating runners to form new leaf rosettes which go

on to become separate plants. Look with binoculars if the plants are not close to the water's edge.

WHEN TO GO The small leaves appear in June as the water warms up and the flowers in July and August, most profusely in hot summers.

WHERE TO GO Ponds, ditches and sheltered margins of lakes and canals, in very clean, fresh water.

SCIENCE STUFF

THERE IS NOTHING TO BE SEEN OF FROGBIT AFTER SEEDS HAVE BEEN SET. THE PLANT FORMS A WINTER BUD THAT, HEAVY WITH STARCH, SINKS TO THE BOTTOM MUD TO WAIT OUT THE WINTER. ITS SUPPLY OF STARCH IS USED TO FORM A NEW ROSETTE THAT RISES TO THE SURFACE AGAIN THE FOLLOWING SPRING.

Water Mint

The commonest wild mint found in Britain, walk through any waterside meadow in summer and the smell of Water Mint will accompany you.

Usually about 30cm tall, sometimes more.

LOOK FOR Egg-shaped clusters of pale purple flowers at the tip of the stem, with rings (whorls) of flowers at intervals below. The leaves are placed opposite each other. The very minty scent can be obvious, even when just walking amongst them, but rub a leaf

between your fingers to really release the strong smell. Water Mint often grows straggling amongst other plants in a tangle of leaves and flowers, and its flowers are sought after by a variety of insects.

WHEN TO GO In flower from July to October.

WHERE TO GO Marshes, wet meadows and the margins of streams, rivers, canals, lakes and ponds.

TOP TIP ★ There are several other purplish flowering plants growing in similar habitats that could be confused with Water Mint.

CORN MINT

MARSH WOUNDWORT

HEDGE WOUNDWORT

COAST

Great Britain is made up of several islands and has over 16,000km of extremely varied coastline. We all love visits to the seaside and immediately know that we are somewhere special. We love the sea itself, the sand, the rock pools and saltmarshes. What makes these areas special is the variety of wildlife to be seen. Coastal plants and animals can be so different to those inland; they have to deal with the combination of wind, waves and a variety of challenging landscapes. The quest for the fifty species on the following pages will take you to a wide range of wonderful places – a visit to the coast will never be the same again. One group of very highly scoring species, the oil beetles (p.168), that you will have to search for early in the year.

Those habitats most influenced by the sea include river estuaries, saltmarshes, shingle banks, sand dunes, rocky cliffs and beaches. These are really exciting places, being some of the most natural habitats that can be visited; untouched by development or agriculture they are as 'natural' as the rainforests of Borneo or the Amazon.

Estuarine habitats

Estuaries occur where the sea meets a river flowing from the land and have a variety of naturally formed coastal habitats.

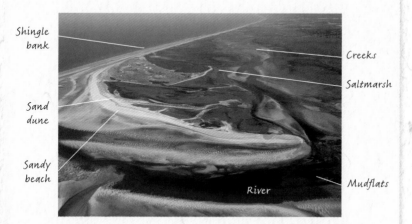

Shingle bank

Creeks

Saltmarsh

Sand dune

Sandy beach

River

Mudflats

Villages and towns beside the sea are good places to start exploring estuarine habitats. Harbours and their surrounding mud or shingle beaches attract gulls at all times of the year and when the tide goes out, seaweeds, shells and other debris are stranded. Look on a map and find footpaths that will take you out past sea walls to sand dunes, shingle banks and saltmarshes, well away from the crowds for some of the best wildlife experiences.

Mud

All is revealed when the tide goes out. Rivers and streams carry silt and soil downstream, and this is deposited at the mouth of the river where the water slows as it meets the sea to form an estuary. The mud is rich in nutrients and, covered by each tide, the nutrients are constantly replenished. Mud is full of life, home to vast numbers of cockles, clams and other molluscs, worms and many other invertebrates, creating a 'larder' that is used all year round by huge flocks of birds. It is a dynamic system, and the mud banks and their inhabitants move around on a regular basis. Explore when the tide is out, but watch out for the tide turning, and for deep pools and soft, sinking mud.

Understanding tides

One important factor that affects life at the coast is the tide, the constant ebb and flow of the sea. You need to know about the tides and what they mean to days out on the beach. Get it wrong and, at best, you could be disappointed; at worst, you could find yourself stranded and in danger.

Tides are caused by the gravitational pull of the moon and the sun. There are two high tides and two low tides every 24 hours. Importantly, the height of these tides varies. When the moon and the sun both pull in the same direction, the high tides are very high and the low tides very low; these are known as 'spring tides' and occur every fortnight around the new moon and the full moon (thus if you note the phase of the moon you will be able to roughly predict the height of the tides). When the moon is opposed by the sun, the sea neither rises so high nor falls so low; these are known as 'neap tides' and occur at the first and third quarters of the moon.

If you are looking for creatures in the rock pools, or in the sand and mud, you need to visit at low tide. The fortnightly spring tides, when the low tides are particularly low, are the best, and the period around the autumn equinox, when some of the lowest tides of the year occur, the very best of all.

Tide tables are produced for all coastal resorts and will help you to plan your visit by telling you the times of the high and low tides on a daily basis. Try to get tide tables that show the height of the tides, as this enables you to really pinpoint the best times for exploration.

Saltmarsh

The British Isles have some of the most important areas of saltmarsh in the world, providing homes for plants and animals that are particularly well adapted to a salty environment.

In estuaries, and where the coast is protected by islands, sand bars and shingle spits, the water is calm enough for mud and sand to be deposited in large quantities, and plants soon start to colonise. The first are tough pioneers like Marsh Samphire (p.180), but others follow and their roots hold the mud together, increasing its stability and soon there is a huge cushion of vegetation protecting the land behind. Due to variations in the height of the mud, and in the height of the tides, some parts of the saltmarsh will be covered by the sea twice a day, while other may only be flooded by the fortnightly spring tides, or even just once or twice a year. This produces a fascinating range of microhabitats. On the lower saltmarsh look for Sea Lavender (p.181), on the higher, drier saltmarsh look for Sea Wormwood (p.145) and roosting waders (p.183).

When exploring saltmarsh be prepared to get muddy, watch out for hidden creeks and pools, and always be aware of the state of the tide, allowing plenty of time to return to dry land before the tide comes in.

Zonation of the shore

As the tide goes out, different areas of the beach will be uncovered and animals and plants (in the form of seaweeds), have exploited these varying and environmentally, harsh niches. Generally divided as follows, all zones may not be visible on all beaches.

SPLASH ZONE   Areas affected by salt spray only. Visible signs on steep rocky cliffs are mainly in the form of lichens.

UPPER SHORE   Area above average high water mark so only covered by the highest spring tides. The driest part of the saltmarsh, sand dunes, the highest point of a shingle bank or rocks.

MIDDLE SHORE   Areas exposed by every tide. Great place to become familiar with creatures that can withstand some drying out as well as those deeper sea creatures caught in the rock pools. On sandy beaches this area may remain wet all the time.

LOWER SHORE   Areas only exposed by the lowest of spring tides. The place to find some of Britin's truly marine animals.

Shingle

Pebble and boulder beaches occur all around the coast. Rocky cliffs are eroded by the sea and the debris smashed up; the size of the resultant pebbles can vary enormously, from fine shingle to large rocks, all rounded by the constant action of the waves. The sea then moves the shingle around, spreading it along the coast and depositing it in select places – often around the mouth of an estuary. This wave action means that shingle and pebble beaches are unstable and usually almost bare of vegetation, but they are superb areas for walking, watching sea birds and seals out at sea, and for beachcombing.

On the higher areas of a shingle beach and perhaps only disturbed by the tide on very stormy days, vegetation of various kinds can survive, but it is tough. The plants have to be specially adapted to conserve water in the face of wind and salt spray: look for their in-rolled, fleshy, spiny or tiny leaves, and for plants that hug the ground. The iconic flower of shingle banks is the Yellow-horned Poppy (p.177). Insect and bird life is usually good here too so do not forget to explore.

Sand

Over a quarter of beaches are sandy. Sand is made up of tiny pieces of rock and shell, and a very specialised group of animals have adapted to life buried in the sand, hidden away from predators and the hostile environment of a windswept beach.

At first a sandy beach may seem empty, and

Beachcombing on the strandline

Nearly all beaches have a strandline – the line of debris, both man-made and natural, left behind when the tide goes out. The strandline is replenished twice each day and moves up and down the beach according to the height of the tide, while big storms will leave their own strandline, often well above the current line of debris. Make a point of looking along the strandline and make a special journey after stormy weather when the strand line can come up with surprising treasures. Different areas of our coast and different times of year will produce different creatures, so never think that you have seen it all. Do be careful though and look before you touch: some items may not be the sort of thing you want to pick up and show your friends!

searching for life can be challenging – look for pools around groynes or where the beach meets rocks and headlands, and visit on a spring tide. On quieter beaches, watch wading birds as they feed; they will show you that there is a lot of life down there somewhere: not only various shells but also tiny worms and other invertebrates, living between the grains. Learn to recognise the telltale signs – worm casts on the sand, tiny protruding siphons. Most beaches also have a satisfying strandline and, especially after storms, a walk along the sand will reveal a variety of washed up creatures.

Sand dunes

On exposed coasts sand is blown along the beach. When it hits something, perhaps debris washed up by the sea or vegetation, the particles of sand are stopped and tiny mounds form. Over time, these mounds may grow to form sand dunes. Salt-tolerant plants such as Marram (p.139) live on the younger dunes closest to the sea, helping to bind the sand together. Older dunes, usually on the landward side of the grassy fore-dunes, support a wider range of plants and there are often low-lying wet areas between the ridges, known as dune slacks. Sheltered from the wind, they are wonderful places to explore and can produce surprises at any time of year; indeed, dunes are some of the best places to see a range of really attractive flowers and butterflies.

Cliff habitats

Cliffs mark the point where the land ends and the sea begins. A fascinating introduction to geology, they show how different rocks are laid down, one on top of each-other and often twisted and contorted to form the landscape, while weathering and erosion caused by the actions of wind, rain and wave forms bays, caves, arches and landslides. There are many coastal footpaths and you can enjoy a bracing walk along the cliff top at any time of year, enjoying these great places not only for their scenic views but also their wildlife – birds, plants and marine mammals.

Rocky cliffs

The north and west coasts of Britain have some of our most dramatic coastal scenery. With long stretches of rocky coast and many offshore islands, they have some of the highest and steepest cliffs. Study a map of the area you are going to visit. Contour lines packed closely together indicate steep, impassable cliffs. Where these have suitable ledges, they are home to breeding seabirds; check the map for footpaths along the cliff top. Stretches where the contours are further apart indicate that the rocks slope more gently down to the beach and here may be colonised by

interesting plants and insects, as well as Puffins (p.163). There may be a good beach at the foot of the cliffs, but the base of others may be pounded by the sea for much of the time and little can establish; you may find some salt-tolerant lichens and an adventurous limpet (but always check the state of the tide, or you may be cut off).

Soft cliffs

Soft cliffs occur all around the coast. They are made up of mud, clay or sand, typically Ice Age deposits that sit on top of harder rocks. Soft cliffs are very vulnerable to erosion, however, and landslides are not uncommon; beware! From below, the sea gnaws away at their base. From above, rain water seeps through the ground, often forming springs and seepages, and after heavy rain can literally lubricate the movement of the ground, causing it to slump. Soft cliffs are great places to look for plants, uncommon invertebrates and hole-nesting birds, but take care on the steep and often wet and slippery slopes. The foot of the cliffs and the beach below can be some of the very best places to look for fossils, such as belemnites (p.153).

Cliff tops

The simple pleasures of a cliff top walk include nodding wild flowers, seabirds zooming past, the Skylark's song and the constant wind. Even where the surrounding land is farmed, many cliffs have a fringing strip of wilderness on the shallow soils over hard, rocky cliffs or the free-draining sands of soft cliffs. Here you will find wild flowers in a beautiful meadow-like turf, with patches of bare ground, the haunts of many bees and beetles. Around a large part of Britain there are cliff top footpaths, beginning in towns and villages and often part of a long distance walk, making access easy. Leave the car parks and cafes behind and you may find that you are the only people there and the coast before you can be yours for the day.

Rock pools

When the tide goes out, the intertidal zone is revealed and on some beaches rock pools are exposed. These are full of life and rock pooling can be very rewarding at any time of year. As well as their own special creatures, rock pools support plants and animals that are otherwise found in deeper water, such as sea slugs (p.159) and give us the chance to see creatures that would only be found by scuba diving. Rock pools have many different niches or microhabitats and it is worth looking carefully at each of them: the shallow sea; pools amongst rocks; sandy pools; under solid rock overhangs; spaces between rocks; under loose rocks; and under seaweed.

The tide uncovers the rock pools twice a day, day after day, and every time they are exposed you may find different species. The best time to search is undoubtedly when the tides are especially low on a spring tide, when you should head to the rocky areas closest to the sea. Do remember, however, that as the tide uncovers the rocks twice a day, it will also cover them up, so a local tide table is essential. Keep an eye out, and when the tide has turned and the sea begins to move back to the shore, so should you.

Related coastal habitats

SALTWATER LAGOONS AND POOLS Usually found close to the sea, just behind a shingle bank or beach, saline lagoons form the backbone of many coastal nature reserves and are great places to visit to see a wide range of birds. If you can, take a closer look into the smaller pools too, as they often support some very specialised plants and animals.

REED BEDS AND FRESHWATER POOLS On low-lying land near the sea, but protected from the influence of salt water except in very severe storms, these areas are wonderful to explore for their variety of life, especially birds. Again, many are part of a nature reserve, so look for boardwalks and footpaths giving access to hides and viewpoints.

GRAZING MARSHES Over the years large areas of mudflat and saltmarsh have been reclaimed from the sea. Now, lying behind seawalls and earthen banks, there may be extensive grazing marshes. Often remote, these can be explored via footpaths and tracks, or viewed from the seawall. Many birds and insects live in these areas, especially the reed-fringed dykes that crisscross the marsh and the rough grassland and bramble clumps along the seawalls.

ARABLE FIELDS Arable fields close to the coast often support a variety of arable weeds. Skylarks and birds of prey nest in them and if stubble is left over the winter this can provide good habitat for many small birds. Sugar beet, commonly grown in the east of Britain, is important for the tens of thousands of Pink-footed Geese that migrate to Britain from Iceland in the winter and feed on the cut tops of the harvested beet.

The seashore code

• Always put rocks and boulders back where you found them, the right way up.
• Handle creatures with care and respect and put them back where you found them.
• Walk carefully through rock pools.
• Make sure any shells you take home are empty.
• Do not leave any animal in a bucket or tray for too long, as the water will become too warm.

The Great British Wildlife Hunt

5

Oystercatcher

One of the noisiest birds of the coast, its shrill, piping calls provide a constant companionable chatter against the background of crashing waves.

Males and females look the same.

LOOK FOR One of the commonest waders, and easy to pick out with its striking black and white plumage, long, orange-red bill and pinkish-red legs. Often very volatile, one minute Oystercatchers are feeding quietly at the water's edge, the next minute they will be running around, chasing each other, eventually flying off, circling and landing again, calling all the time.

WHEN TO GO Present all year round – the breeding season is from March to May. At high tide they can be found roosting on rocks, sea walls and nearby fields, sometimes in large numbers, often with their bills tucked up under their wings.

WHERE TO GO Found in almost all coastal habitats. Breeds on shingle banks, rocky beaches, sand dunes, saltmarshes and grassy cliff tops and islands. Oystercatchers will also nest inland, beside rivers and in agricultural fields. In winter you will find them on mudflats and estuaries.

SCIENCE STUFF

OYSTERCATCHERS DO NOT EAT OYSTERS BUT DO CONSUME LOTS OF MUSSELS AND COCKLES, MUCH TO THE DISPLEASURE OF MUSSEL AND COCKLE-FISHERMEN.

The Great British Wildlife Hunt

10

Starfish

A group of starfish is known as a 'galaxy', and any one of the several species that occur around British coasts is a great find on a beach holiday.

Common Starfish

The classic seaside starfish, widespread around the coast. Up to 15cm across.

Spiny Starfish

A monstrous, armour-plated starfish found on the south and west coasts. Up to 30cm.

Common Brittlestar

Found on all coasts. Up to 4cm.

Cushion Starfish

Small, and only found in the south and west of the country. Up to 2cm across.

Sunstar

Lives in deeper water.

With their (usually) five arms, starfish are easy to identify. Each arm has many tubular 'feet' on the underside – watch them glide effortlessly over the rocks and sand.

WHEN TO GO All these starfish can be found during the summer months. After storms, especially in the winter, look for them washed up on the tide line.

WHERE TO GO Rock pools at low tide. Look under ledges and between and under loose rocks. Common Starfish prefer sandy beaches and can sometimes be found tucked under the groynes. Sunstars are mostly found washed up dead on the tide line.

SCIENCE STUFF

YOU MAY FIND STARFISH WITH FEWER THAN FIVE ARMS, AS THEY ARE EASILY DAMAGED (A REASON TO TREAT THEM GENTLY). THE ARMS WILL GROW BACK, HOWEVER, AND AMAZINGLY, IN SOME CASES A WHOLE NEW STARFISH CAN GROW FROM A LOST ARM, BECAUSE ALMOST ALL THE VITAL ORGANS ARE LOCATED IN THE ARMS.

The Great British Wildlife Hunt
15

Sea wracks

These brown seaweeds may look rather similar, but they can be identified quite easily, and it is fun to try to find all five on the same beach.

Upper shore sea wracks

Spiral Wrack

These swollen areas are reproductive organs —

Has twisted fronds with an obvious midrib. No air bladders. Looks like a dangling 'bunch of keys'.

Channelled Wrack

Found in short, bushy clumps attached to rocks. No air bladders.

Lower shore sea wracks

Bladder Wrack

The commonest species. Forked fronds with a midrib and many pairs of air bladders.

Egg Wrack

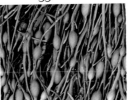

Long, narrow fronds without a midrib, but with single large, egg-shaped air bladders.

Serrated Wrack

Flattened fronds with a midrib and serrated edges. No air bladders.

WHEN TO GO Any time of the year when the tide is out. Sometimes every available surface is covered by one or more of these seaweeds.

WHERE TO GO Rocky beaches, wooden sea defences and rocky cliffs.

• •

NEWS EXTRA! The differences between these seaweeds involve size, the presence or absence of a midrib, and the presence of air bladders (which help them float). Do not mistake the pairs of swollen reproductive bodies at the tips of the fronds for air bladders. The Egg Wrack's reproductive bodies develop on the sides of the fronds and look like lollipops. Egg Wrack only produces one air bladder each year, so you can tell how old the seaweed is – and they can live for many years.

Turnstone

Don't overlook this small but confiding wader – once the day trippers have gone at the end of the day Turnstones may fly on to the beach to check out the chip wrappers!

Smart breeding plumage.

Short bill and orange legs.

LOOK FOR A small but chunky, well-marked wader. Turnstones are usually found in small flocks, keeping up a conversational rattling chatter as they fly around. The stone-turning habit that gives them their name makes them stand out from the crowd – watch and see them turn over quite large stones. They also rummage in piles of seaweed on the strandline, looking for sand hoppers, insects, shellfish and fish remains. They can be quite bold and may become quite tolerant of people – a delightful highlight of a seaside holiday.

WHEN TO GO The greatest numbers are present in winter and on migration and they are most obvious from August through the winter to May. Most move north in summer to breed in Scandinavia, but a few may stay for the summer.

WHERE TO GO Seaweed-covered rocks, muddy estuaries and sandy and pebbly beaches with seaweed and other debris along the strandline. Turnstones are also sometimes found on promenades, car parks and even lawns and roadside verges by the sea.

TOP TIP ✶ In flight the bold black and white patterns are obvious and separate Turnstones from other common shoreline waders.

The Great British Wildlife Hunt
15

Curlew

The Curlew calls its name as it flies, a mournful 'coor-li', and this, together with its bubbling, trilling song, is evocative of wild saltmarshes and moorland.

Females have the longest bills

LOOK FOR The very long, down-curved bill, which is obvious, both in flight and when wading in shallow water or mud as it probes for molluscs and crabs. The plumage is rather drab, a streaky mixture of greys and browns, but Curlews are generally shy and can be difficult to see close up.

WHEN TO GO Although present all year round, the greatest numbers are found on the coast in winter.

WHERE TO GO Congregates in large flocks on estuaries and mudflats, roosting on higher ground at high tides, or feeding in wet fields and grazing marshes just inland of the sea wall. In spring and early summer, most move to the breeding grounds on upland moors and bogs, with only small, scattered populations in the lowlands, on meadows and grassy heathland.

SCIENCE STUFF

WADING BIRDS HAVE BILLS OF DIFFERENT LENGTHS, ALLOWING THEM TO REACH FOOD AT VARIOUS OF DEPTHS IN THE MUD. THIS MEANS THAT LOTS OF DIFFERENT BIRDS CAN LIVE TOGETHER IN FOOD-RICH COASTAL ESTUARIES WITHOUT COMPETING FOR FOOD.

CURLEW

BLACK-TAILED GODWIT

REDSHANK

KNOT

The Great British Wildlife Hunt

15

Marram Grass

Sand dunes and Marram Grass are always found together. The sharp points at the tips of the Marram stems will be obvious to those foolhardy enough to go without shoes!

LOOK FOR Large, dense tussocks of straw-coloured leaves, often rather dead-looking. The tips of the leaves are sharp, making shoes essential on the dunes. The leaves roll inwards in dry weather to help the plant to retain water; despite the proximity of the sea, dunes are dry, thirsty places for plants.

WHEN TO GO Present all year round. The flowers – long cylindrical spikes – appear in July and August.

WHERE TO GO Sand dunes close to the sea, generally the younger, more recently-formed dunes.

NEWS EXTRA! Marram has the ability to grow upwards when buried by sand, and its roots and shoots help to bind the sand together and form the first dunes. Lyme Grass and Sand Couch are two other grasses that help to hold the sand together, but neither can help to produce large dunes in the same way as the deeply buried stems and old matted roots of Marram.

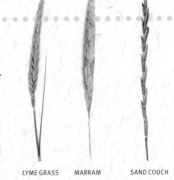

LYME GRASS   MARRAM   SAND COUCH

Ringed Plover

This little wader gives itself away with its characteristic stop-start feeding action. Watch it quickly run and then abruptly stop as it searches the shoreline for sand hoppers and insects.

Males and females are similar.

LOOK FOR A small, sandy-brown wader with a characteristic facial pattern, but well camouflaged on the shingle beaches where it breeds. The bill is short and stubby, and turns blackish in winter. Do not go too close – Ringed Plovers will quickly fly to a more distant spot when disturbed. The Little Ringed Plover is very similar, but has a narrow golden eye ring and is a bird of freshwater habitats.

WHEN TO GO Present all year round. Ringed Plovers can have two broods a year so are rarely away from their breeding areas in summer. Numbers increase in spring and autumn as birds breeding further north stop off in Britain on their way south, while others come here for the winter.

WHERE TO GO Sandy and shingle beaches away from busy areas. In winter, they can also be found feeding with other waders around estuaries and mudflats.

SCIENCE STUFF

LIKE MANY OTHER BIRDS, ADULT RINGED PLOVERS WILL PERFORM A 'BROKEN WING' DISTRACTION DISPLAY TO LURE PREDATORS AWAY FROM THEIR NEST AND CHICKS. ONCE THE PREDATOR HAS CHANGED TACK TO CHASE THE APPARENTLY HELPLESS ADULT, IT FLIES OFF.

Mermaid's purse

A delightful find for a beachcomber, although everyone wonders what they are! These are the egg cases of two common fish, the Dogfish and the Spotted Ray.

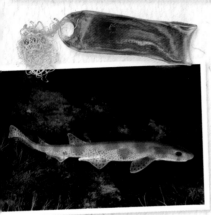

DOGFISH

SPOTTED RAY

Dogfish

LOOK FOR Pale brown, swollen bladders, longer than they are wide, but rarely more than 6cm long, with curly tendrils at the corners. The tendrils wrap around seaweed and rocks, anchoring the egg case to the shore until the young fish hatch out, after which the used bladders become brittle and are washed away. Adult Dogfish are spotted and can reach a metre in length. It is not uncommon to find the adults washed up dead on the shore. They are mostly in bits, but sometimes you'll find whole fish – if the gulls have not yet found them.

Spotted Ray

LOOK FOR Blue-black bladders, up to 10cm long and tough and leathery in texture. The centre is bulbous and the corners long and drawn-out, but without tendrils. (The egg cases of some skates are very similar, and they cannot easily be told apart.)

WHEN TO GO All year round, but especially after stormy weather.

WHERE TO GO The strandline of any beach, or indeed anywhere where debris from the sea is washed up. Shingle beaches are particularly good hunting grounds.

The Great British Wildlife Hunt
35

Spoonbill

This unique and bizarre bird is scarce in Britain, but a Spoonbill will add a touch of Mediterranean glamour to any coastal marsh that it visits.

Dark bill with yellow tip (juveniles have an all-dark bill).

LOOK FOR A large, white heron-like bird with an amazing spoon-shaped bill that it sweeps from side to side when feeding. The special shape scoops and filters the water, trapping small fish, molluscs and crustaceans inside. If seen well, look for the shaggy crest and yellow breast band on breeding birds. Spoonbills often loaf around for long periods with their bill tucked under a wing, but be patient and wait for them to begin feeding.

WHEN TO GO Small numbers occur through the summer months, with just a few staying the winter. On estuaries and mudflats they join other waders and herons, flying to and fro as the tides rise and fall.

WHERE TO GO Mudflats, estuaries and coastal lagoons. They can appear anywhere around the coast, and have recently returned to Britain as a breeding bird in Norfolk. Rare inland.

TOP TIP ★ Smaller than a Grey Heron. In flight the bill, head and neck are held extended (herons and egrets usually fly with their neck drawn in, in an S-shape).

GREY HERON

SPOONBILL

Sea anemones

The Great British Wildlife Hunt · **10**

These exotic rock-pool creatures are animals not plants. Their tentacles contain many stinging cells, and although they will not hurt, it is wise not to poke them with your fingers.

Strawberry Anemone

Beadlet Anemone

This is a selection of the commonest anemones to be found in rock pools. If you are lucky, you may find others.

Similar to the Beadlet Anemone but found along the south coast only.

Common on any rocky shore. May be red or green.

Snakelocks Anemone

Common on all southern and western coasts. Its ground colour is grey, but it looks green due to the presence of an algae that lives inside it.

Gem Anemone

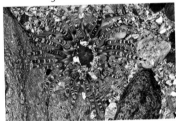

Found around the coasts of south-west England and Wales. Often hard to spot as it is usually partly buried in the sand.

WHEN TO GO All year round, but time your visit to coincide with one of the lowest tides (which occur every fortnight).

WHERE TO GO Rock pools from the upper shore to the sea. Look under stones, on rock ledges and seaweed. Some, like the Gem Anemone, prefer sandy or gritty beaches.

SCIENCE STUFF

BEADLET ANEMONES CAN BE LEFT HIGH AND DRY BY THE FALLING TIDE AND WHEN OUT OF THE WATER APPEAR AS JELLY-LIKE RED BLOBS (THEIR TENTACLES ARE FOLDED INSIDE TO HELP RETAIN MOISTURE). MOST OTHER SPECIES OF ANEMONE OCCUR ON THE LOWER SHORE OR IN DEEPER WATER BECAUSE THEY DO NOT HAVE THE SAME ABILITY TO PROTECT THEMSELVES FROM DRYING OUT.

The Great British Wildlife Hunt
5

Herring Gull

Surely the number one sound of the seaside, the loud yelping wails of the Herring Gull resonate around every coastal town and are every seaside camper's wake-up call.

Typical view of Herring Gull.

LOOK FOR One of the largest of the gulls, with a grey back, fierce expression due to its pale eye, a yellow bill and wonderful pink legs. In winter the head is much duller, with dark smudges. Immature birds tend to be brown and streaky, and it takes them three or four years to attain adult plumage.

WHEN TO GO Present all year round. Herring Gulls breed around most coastlines and numbers increase in the winter, as birds from Scandinavia and Russia join our resident population.

WHERE TO GO Beaches, harbours and seaside towns. Nesting sites tend to be on grassy or rocky cliffs and also often on buildings.

NEWS EXTRA! Herring Gulls can be quite alarming when they swoop down and steal your ice cream or chips, and in some seaside towns signs are put up warning you about this cheeky behaviour. When they get so close you can see how big they really are.

The Great British Wildlife Hunt
20

Sea Wormwood

Not the most attractive name for this delicate, aromatic plant – the best thing about **Sea Wormwood** is its scent. A piece behind the ear is thought to keep flies away.

Stems up to 50cm tall.

SMALL YELLOW FLOWERS
IN LATE SUMMER

LOOK FOR Leaves divided into narrow segments and densely covered with silky-white hairs, making the whole plant look silvery. Sea Wormwood is the only silvery-grey, feathery-leaved plant on the saltmarsh (Sea Purslane has greyish leaves, but they are spoon-shaped). The flowers are tiny, yellowish and grouped into small clusters (they are wind-pollinated so do not have to be big and showy).

WHEN TO GO The distinctive leaves appear from around April, and the flowers in August and September.

WHERE TO GO Saltmarshes, especially the slightly higher zones alongside channels and narrow saltmarsh 'gutters', and also along the landward edge of the saltmarsh, including the base of sea walls.

NEWS EXTRA! The strong lavender-like odour led to the use of Sea Wormwood as a strewing herb: the foliage was scattered on floors to drive out fleas and lice from medieval dwellings.

The Great British Wildlife Hunt
15

Cuttlefish bone

This 'bone' is the internal shell of the Cuttlefish –
a squid-like creature that is one of the most specialised
molluscs (a huge group that includes slugs and snails).

Up to 15cm long.

CUTTLEFISH

SQUID

LOOK FOR White, oval shapes that clearly stand out from the sand, shingle and other debris. The 'bone' is a soft pumice-like material, made up mostly of calcium. Live Cuttlefish will not be found on the beach.

WHEN TO GO After the high tide, when the strand line of debris along the top of the beach is obvious. Commonest in the winter months but worth looking for after any rough or stormy weather.

WHERE TO GO Cuttlefish mostly live on sandy or muddy-bottomed seas. Their 'bones' can be found washed up on sand or shingle beaches.

SCIENCE STUFF

CUTTLEFISH AND SQUID ARE CLOSELY RELATED, ALTHOUGH A CUTTLEFISH IS ONLY HALF THE SIZE OF A SQUID. BOTH SQUIRT A CLOUD OF BLACK 'INK' INTO THE WATER TO DETER PREDATORS. THE CUTTLEFISH MOVES AROUND THE OCEAN FLOOR AND ITS UNIQUE 'BONE' IS FILLED WITH GAS, WHICH HELPS THE CUTTLEFISH TO CONTROL ITS POSITION IN THE WATER. THE SQUID HAS ONLY A THIN INTERNAL SKELETON (KNOWN AS A 'PEN') AND DOES NOT REQUIRE SUCH A PRECISE POSITIONING SYSTEM AS IT ROAMS FREELY.

Shelduck

A common and conspicuous piebald bird that is halfway between a duck and a goose – its bold and striking pattern makes it recognisable over a long distance.

Male

Female

LOOK FOR Distinctive and colourful, about the size of a small goose, the Shelduck is mainly white with a green head, russet brown 'scarf' and red bill. Males have a knob on the bill. Commonly seen in pairs, up-ending in shallow pools or dabbling in mud.

WHEN TO GO Present all year round, although from July to October many leave Britain to moult in Germany. Others remain and form large flocks in some of our bigger

estuaries, especially Bridgewater Bay in Somerset, where as many as 4000 can sometimes be seen together.

WHERE TO GO Estuaries and sheltered coasts with lagoons and mudflats. It nests in rabbit burrows, old tree-trunks and other holes and cracks, and during the breeding season you may also find it on dunes and coastal grassland, as well as inland.

NEWS EXTRA! Females and their young join together to form large groups or 'crèches' to protect the chicks from predators. These nursery schools may contain up to 50 chicks.

Avocet

A bird with plenty of style – and attitude. Watch it defend its space on the marsh – it doesn't look so delicate as it chases away intruders!

LOOK FOR A black and white bird with a long, upturned bill. With binoculars the blue legs can also be seen. Look for it marching through shallow water, sweeping its bill from side to side as it feeds. It can be very feisty too, seeing off all intruders from the nest area, even species of birds that are not a threat to its eggs or chicks.

WHEN TO GO Present all year round. Most breed on the east coast of the UK, where a few remain through the winter, but many move south and west to winter around the sheltered estuaries of the south coast.

WHERE TO GO Sheltered coastal lagoons and shallow saline pools with muddy margins and little vegetation. Avocets breed mostly on nature reserves, where the habitat is often specially managed for them.

NEWS EXTRA! The Avocet is the emblem of the RSPB and a great conservation success story. Extinct in Britain by the mid 19th century, due to habitat loss and egg-collecting, it re-colonised areas of coast deliberately flooded as part of coastal defences during the Second World War. Now there are more than 1,000 breeding pairs.

Edible Cockle

A single cockle sitting in the drying sand of an ebbing tide is perfection – but it is never alone and will have thousands of relatives hiding close by.

Up to 5cm across.

LOOK FOR Beautifully formed, rounded shells, sitting on the surface or half-buried in sand or mud. They are typical bivalve molluscs (two-shelled sea-snails) and are superbly well adapted to their intertidal lifestyle. They have a strong 'foot' that they use to anchor themselves in the sand and are rarely dislodged by waves. Cockles usually occur in large 'beds'. If you find a stranded cockle on the sand, place it in a shallow pool and watch it dig itself back into the sand.

WHEN TO GO Present all year round. Wait for the tide to go out – live ones can sometimes then be left stranded on the sand.

WHERE TO GO Find muddy and sandy beaches and search between the middle and lower shore. Look also in the soft mud of estuaries.

SCIENCE STUFF

COCKLES ARE IMPORTANT AS A FOOD SOURCE FOR PEOPLE, BUT THEY ALSO HAVE A FASCINATING LIFE OF THEIR OWN AND THEIR FAIR SHARE OF NATURAL PREDATORS.

A half-buried cockle with siphon, used for filter feeding.

Cockle shells with holes that have been drilled by a Necklace Shell.

The Great British Wildlife Hunt
10

Sea Lettuce

The fronds of this seaweed can be up to 30cm long but are only two cells thick, making them look like floating green skin.

LOOK FOR Bright green, delicate-looking (but actually very tough) fronds attached to rocks by a holdfast, with the fronds floating in pools or hanging limply over the rocks. The other common, bright green seaweed is Gutweed. This has finger-like fronds and may completely cover rocks, making the surfaces slippery.

WHEN TO GO Present all year round. It can be very abundant in high summer.

WHERE TO GO All kinds of rocky coasts and all areas of the intertidal zone. It can grow into large attractive clumps in the deepest pools that do not dry out. In summer, Sea Lettuce can cover large areas of mudflats but may be grazed off by herbivorous limpets and winkles.

SCIENCE STUFF

THE EDGES OF THE FRONDS MAY LOOK BLEACHED WHITE – REPRODUCTIVE SPORES ARE RELEASED FROM THESE AREAS AND CAN SOMETIMES TURN THE WATER IN A ROCK POOL A CLOUDY LETTUCE-GREEN. THESE BLEACHED FRONDS CAN ALSO BE FOUND WASHED UP ON THE STRANDLINE.

The Great British · Wildlife Hunt

10

Redshank

A typical bird of the saltmarsh and one of the easiest waders to identify, making it a benchmark against which other waders can be compared for identification purposes.

Plumage much greyer in winter.

Orangey-red legs.

Two-toned bill.

Redshank raising the alarm.

White back and white trailing edge to the wing.

LOOK FOR The Redshank is a common bird and is almost always present amongst mixed groups of waders. Although it has long legs, it prefers the shallows and therefore is found around the edges of the water. It is wary and noisy – the watchman of the marsh – alerting all other birds to danger.

WHEN TO GO Present all year round. Very active and noisy when breeding, darting to and fro and calling as it defends its territory.

WHERE TO GO Found on saltmarshes and inland grazing marshes where breeding takes place. At other times of year it stays by the coast around most estuarine habitats: saltmarshes, mudflats and wet fields close by.

TOP TIP ✷ Learn to recognise the calls of the Redshank, which competes with the Oystercatcher for the title 'noisiest bird on the marsh'. Redshanks give a loud *teu-lu, teu-lulu* as they fly, a scolding *teuk* in alarm and yodelling *tu-tu-tu-tu-tu … song*.

The Great British Wildlife Hunt

25

Eider

'Sea ducks' spend a lot of their time at sea and this is one of the most abundant and beautiful species. Eiders nest around northern coasts and are not to be missed.

LOOK FOR Males are handsome, plump, black and white birds, often seen beside brown females. They bob around on choppy waters around rocky coasts and are never far from the sea. Close up, the subtle pastel greens on the head and soft pinks on the breast of males are visible. Eiders are found in pairs during the breeding season, otherwise they are often in family groups, gathering together to form flocks on the sea. They dive under the water for their prey and give a soft crooning call during their courtship display in late winter.

WHEN TO GO Present all year round. They are sociable birds and can be found in huge flocks in winter, especially in the north.

WHERE TO GO Breeds on rocky coasts and islands in northern England, Scotland and Northern Ireland. They are more widespread in winter, and should be looked for along any sheltered rocky coast.

SCIENCE STUFF

EIDERS ARE REPORTED TO BE THE FASTEST BIRD IN STEADY, LEVEL FLIGHT, REACHING AN IMPRESSIVE 47.2MPH (BEING LARGE, HEAVY DUCKS WITH RELATIVELY SMALL WINGS, THEY HAVE TO FLY FAST TO ACHIEVE SUFFICIENT 'LIFT' TO REMAIN AIRBORNE). THEY USE THEIR POWERFUL BILLS TO CRUSH MUSSELS AND CRABS TO EAT, WHILE THEIR BREAST FEATHERS ARE THE SOURCE OF THE ORIGINAL 'EIDERDOWN' USED FOR DUVETS AND SLEEPING BAGS DUE TO ITS FANTASTIC INSULATING PROPERTIES.

Belemnite

Belemnites lived over two hundred million years ago in the age of the dinosaurs. They became extinct at the same time and are now one of the easiest fossils to find.

Belemnites looked very much like modern-day squids.

LOOK FOR Orangey-brown or grey-black bullet-shaped rocks, the fossilised remains of the protective shell of the belemnite. They are usually found lying in rock pools or amongst shingle – sometimes still embedded in the rock. You may be lucky enough to find a whole one, with a point at one end and a small depression at the other. The soft parts of the belemnite, the head, tail and tentacles, are rarely fossilised.

WHEN TO GO Present all year round. New fossils are often exposed after autumn and winter storms.

WHERE TO GO Rock pools and shingle beaches in areas close to rocks of the Jurassic and Cretaceous period, such as chalks and soft mudstones.

SCIENCE STUFF

AREAS KNOWN AS BELEMNITE 'BATTLEFIELDS' HAVE BEEN FOUND (NOTE THE REFERENCE TO THEIR BULLET SHAPE). THESE HAVE MANY HUNDREDS OF BELEMNITES DEPOSITED IN ONE PLACE, THOUGHT TO HAVE BEEN VOMITED OUT BY SHARKS AND ICHTHYOSAURS AFTER THEY CONSUMED THE SOFT PARTS.

Rock Pipit

On the face of it the Rock Pipit is a nondescript and unobtrusive small brown bird, but it will enliven a visit to a rocky coast with its cheerful calls and relative tameness.

Males and females are alike.

LOOK FOR A noisy, small brown bird running to and fro, hopping and taking short flights amongst seaweed-covered boulders and along the tide line, looking for small invertebrate prey. Rock Pipits may be indifferent to your presence and will happily feed close to you if you stand still, giving great views. In early summer, they perch on prominent rocks to launch their parachuting song flight.

WHEN TO GO Resident in Britain and found all year round, but especially obvious when feeding young in June.

WHERE TO GO Breeds only on rocky coasts, around cliffs and boulder-strewn beaches. More widespread in winter, feeding along the strandline of beaches, and in saltmarshes.

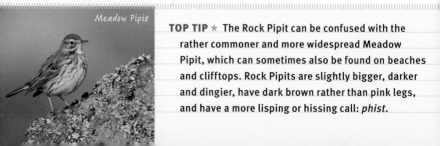

Meadow Pipit

TOP TIP ✲ The Rock Pipit can be confused with the rather commoner and more widespread Meadow Pipit, which can sometimes also be found on beaches and clifftops. Rock Pipits are slightly bigger, darker and dingier, have dark brown rather than pink legs, and have a more lisping or hissing call: *phist*.

The Great British Wildlife Hunt
25

Sea Potato

The shell-like body of this sea urchin, found washed up dead on the sand, is one of my most treasured possessions. You are unlikely to find it alive.

LOOK FOR The delicate remains of the Sea Potato are unmistakable – dirty white with characteristic curved lines of pitted markings where spines used to be. The heart shape gives rise to its other common name, Heart Urchin.

Sea Potatoes live buried in a permanent burrow in the sand, filtering seawater to obtain food. To find a live one you will need a spade. Look for rounded depressions in the sand about 10cm across. Dig down carefully: it may mean a Sea Potato lies 10–15cm beneath the sand. If you find one, remember to put it back gently.

WHEN TO GO Dead specimens are most likely to be washed up in the late summer and autumn. You could be lucky enough to find a live urchin at any time of year.

WHERE TO GO Sheltered sandy beaches on all coasts. Look for the remains freshly washed up on the sand closest to the sea or along the strandline; fragments can be numerous and a complete Sea Potato is a real delight, but be very careful, as they are easily broken.

SCIENCE STUFF

WHEN ALIVE, A SEA POTATO IS COVERED WITH SHORT, YELLOWISH SPINES, WITH TUFTS OF STIFFER, LONGER SPINES AT ONE END. THESE PROTECT IT FROM PREDATORS AND HELP TO GUIDE FOOD PARTICLES TOWARDS THE MOUTH ON THE UNDERSIDE.

Fulmar

Gliding effortlessly along the cliff face or sitting placidly on its precarious nest, this wonderful sea bird will sometimes provide you with great views.

LOOK FOR The stiff-winged flight – long glides with bouts of rapid, shallow flapping. This and their heavier build distinguish them from gulls. Fulmars nest on cliff ledges, usually in colonies, and the adults and young can be spotted sitting together. Pairs mate for life – more than 50 years – and both sexes incubate the eggs and feed the young. The adults remain close to the breeding colonies for most of the year, but immature birds (and Fulmars may not breed until they are nine years old), stay out at sea.

WHEN TO GO Just about any month of the year close to the breeding cliffs. Otherwise, look for them offshore during strong winds in autumn and winter.

WHERE TO GO Sea cliffs with narrow ledges for nesting. In many places Fulmars are the only cliff-nesting sea bird. Out at sea, Fulmars follow trawlers; they are hardly ever seen inland.

SCIENCE STUFF

FULMARS ARE MEMBERS OF THE SAME FAMILY AS ALBATROSSES AND HAVE SIMILAR TUBULAR NOSTRILS ON THE BILL, ADAPTATIONS FOR EXCRETING SALT. THEY CAN ALSO SQUIRT A FISHY, OILY MESS WHEN DISTURBED, AS BIRD RINGERS KNOW TO THEIR COST! NUMBERS HAVE INCREASED SPECTACULARLY; THEY WERE ONCE CONFINED TO THE REMOTE ISLAND OF ST KILDA OFF THE HEBRIDES, BUT HAVE NOW SPREAD TO ALL COASTS, WITH AROUND HALF A MILLION BREEDING PAIRS.

The Great British Wildlife Hunt

25

Common and Grey Seals

When basking on the rocks, seals are shy and wary, but once in the water they are in their element and may suddenly appear in the sea beside you, curious and even almost friendly.

Grey Seal

LOOK FOR A long muzzle with a 'roman' nose. This feature is not obvious in females and young. The fur is blotched brown and grey. Grey Seals may be active and noisy, giving a rather mournful wail that may carry for more than a kilometre over isolated beaches. Pups are born from September to November.

Common Seal

LOOK FOR A rounded head with a dog-like face, recalling a spaniel with long whiskers and 'v' shaped nostrils. The fur is finely spotted grey or brown, and they can be up to two metres long. Pups are born from June to September.

WHEN TO GO All year. Seals rest on rocky shores and sand bars for several hours a day at low tide.

WHERE TO GO Found in all kinds of coastal waters, but commonest on the east coast of England and the north and west of Scotland. Grey Seals outnumber Common Seals by 2:1, preferring rocky coasts in the north and west with a few colonies on the east coast.

TOP TIP ✳ In some locations, both species occur together and they can be tricky to tell apart. Grey seals are generally bigger and darker, although their pups have white fur.

The Great British Wildlife Hunt

25

Peregrine Falcon

Built for speed, Peregrines can reach up to 320kph (200mph) during their hunting 'stoop' and literally knock their prey out of the air.

LOOK FOR When hunting, a Peregrine's turn of speed is incredible, making it hard to follow with binoculars. The broad-based wings and almost anchor-shaped silhouette are more easily seen in level flight or when soaring – they often appear to soar and dive just for fun. Peregrines spend a lot of time sitting on a perch with a good view, allowing their barrel-shaped chest, barred (adult) or streaked (juvenile) underparts and hooded appearance to be clearly seen.

WHEN TO GO Present all year round, but easiest to spot during the breeding season: their aerial displays are obvious in February–March and later in the season both adults fly to and fro bringing in food for the chicks. In autumn and winter they are more nomadic, hunting over marshes and low-lying agricultural land.

WHERE TO GO Tall cliffs, both inland and on the coast, provide nest sites. Otherwise, watch out for Peregrines anywhere there are concentrations of birds, such as estuaries with plenty of waders and ducks, where they can provoke some dramatic, aerial manoeuvres.

A mother and chicks on a Manchester roof.

NEWS EXTRA! Peregrines have successfully spread into towns and cities. Tall buildings provide ample ledges for nesting and there is an endless supply of food in the form of Feral Pigeons and, amazingly, migrating birds caught at night.

The Great British Wildlife Hunt

45

Sea slugs

Related to the slugs in your garden, and other molluscs without a shell, but sea slugs come in gaudy colours and enjoy the fantastic alternative name of 'Nudibranch'.

Sea Lemon

The size and shape of a small lemon, the body is covered with 'warts'. Feeds on breadcrumb sponges.

Green Sea Slug

Up to 4cm long. Sucks the energy-making chloroplasts from green seaweed, allowing it to create its own energy from sunlight.

Grey Sea Slug

Up to 10cm long. Feeds on sea anemones, and absorbs their stinging cells to use for protection.

Doto

Only 10mm long but beautiful. Feeds on hydroids.

WHEN TO GO All year round, but at the lowest tides. They often feed at night, so for an exciting adventure head down to the beach with a torch after dark.

WHERE TO GO Rock pools on the lower shore, especially where there are many submerged rocks, overhangs and seaweed. Look where there are breadcrumb sponges, hydroids, sea anemones and green seaweeds. Sea slugs can also occasionally be found stranded on the tideline.

A breadcrumb sponge – looks like the surface of the moon.

Hydroids – colonial animals related to sea anemones.

TOP TIP ★ Look for sea slugs where you find their prey.

Hermit crab

The only crabs that don't have their own shells. A hermit crab has to find an empty shell, and every so often, as the crab grows it 'moves house' and the shell is changed for a bigger one.

LOOK FOR Shells moving unusually fast. With their original inhabitants inside, shells, in particular in winkles and Topshells, can be seen moving but tend to glide over the surface. Hermit crabs scurry, and when disturbed, will stop and withdraw into the shell, closing the entrance with the large right pincer. The soft body is rarely seen; it coils around to fit the shape of its second-hand shell. Small crabs live in the shells of periwinkles, topshells or Dog Whelks, adult hermit crabs almost always use the shells of Common Whelks.

WHEN TO GO All year round but, as with other crabs, they can remain in deeper water in the depths of winter. The summer months are generally the best times for rock pooling.

WHERE TO GO Rock pools exposed by the tide. Hermit crabs may be seen moving from pools that are drying out to those still full of water further down the shore.

SCIENCE STUFF

HERMIT CRABS AND SEA ANEMONES CAN HAVE A MUTUALLY BENEFICIAL RELATIONSHIP. THE SEA ANEMONE HELPS TO PROTECT THE CRAB FROM PREDATORS, AND BENEFITS FROM SCRAPS OF FOOD DROPPED BY THE CRAB, WHICH IS A MESSY EATER.

The Great British Wildlife Hunt

40

Bottle-nosed Dolphin

What a thrill to see a dolphin in the seas around Britain! They can be watched from boats, but this inshore species can also be spotted from land – regularly in some favoured places.

LOOK FOR Bottle-nosed Dolphins are social animals and occur in groups ('pods') of about ten. There may be lots of activity, with leaps and somersaults, but when they are cruising just below the surface look for the tall dorsal fin, centrally placed along the back, short nose and the 'smiley' mouth line.

WHEN TO GO Present all year round. Go to favoured spots when the sea is calm as there is a better chance of spotting them without large, foam-crested waves to confuse you.

WHERE TO GO Large bays and estuaries, also around islands in the north and west of Britain. Coastal cliffs make a good vantage point. Breeding populations occur in the Moray Firth in Scotland and Cardigan Bay in Wales.

TOP TIP ∗ Once dolphins are spotted, use binoculars for a closer look. Bottle-nosed Dolphins are grey all over; if you see any dark and light markings you are probably looking at Common Dolphins, which are occasionally seen inshore when hunting Mackerel or Herring.

The Great British Wildlife Hunt

15

Jellyfish

Although thought of as creatures of warm seas, several jellyfish occur in the cooler waters around our coasts. This is a selection of those regularly found stranded on the beach.

Moon Jellyfish

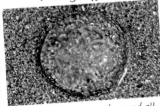

Up to 50cm across. Found around all coasts. Not powerful enough to sting.

Compass Jellyfish

Up to 20cm across. May occur in large swarms following plankton blooms in the sea. Has a powerful sting.

Dustbin-lid Jellyfish

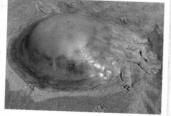

Up to 90cm across. No sting but tentacles can still cause a rash.

Lion's Mane Jellyfish

Scarce but very colourful. A large species, more than 50cm across, with a powerful sting even when stranded.

LOOK FOR Almost clear, jelly-like circles on the sand. Each species shows different markings and they can be very colourful. Most jellyfish have stinging cells in their tentacles, but not all are powerful enough to sting a human. It is always best, however, to avoid skin contact with their tentacles, dead or alive.

WHEN TO GO Any time of year, but especially after storms in autumn. They are often stranded at low tide.

WHERE TO GO Usually seen washed up on the beach, often on the strandline.

NEWS EXTRA! Spectacular swarms may be found in the sea in late summer, in sheltered bays, harbours and estuaries.

The Great British Wildlife Hunt

25

Puffin

One of the most recognisable birds in Britain, the comical bill and behaviour of the Puffin make it a firm favourite and a bird that everyone wants to see.

LOOK FOR The black and white plumage and multicoloured bill are unmistakable. Visit one of its coastal colonies, find a clifftop vantage point and watch with binoculars for groups of Puffins sitting on the sea just offshore or flying past with very fast wingbeats that can almost seem a blur. Well worth the trip.

WHEN TO GO They are summer visitors, arriving in March and leaving in late August. They disappear out to sea for the rest of the year.

WHERE TO GO Nearly always seen close to their breeding colonies, situated on grassy cliff top slopes, or flying to and fro over the sea. Very scarce in the south-east and almost unknown inland.

TOP TIP ★ Steep, grassy cliffs are dangerous places, especially when riddled with Puffin burrows and rocky crevices. Observe from a safe distance, or from the beach if possible. At some colonies boat trips are on offer, allowing some really close views.

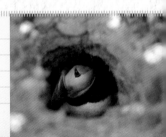

The Great British Wildlife Hunt
10

Razor clam

Empty razor shells are common on the strandline and sometimes litter beaches in their thousands. Finding a living razor clam is much more of a challenge.

Up to 20cm long.

LOOK FOR Razor shells are easily recognised by their elongated shape. Razor clams live in the sand and are extremely well adapted to this habitat. They move away from danger exceedingly quickly, shooting down into their tube-shaped burrows, helped by the smooth, shiny surface of their shell. At the same time, a jet of water is ejected and it is this jet, together with a small keyhole-shaped depression in the sand (caused by the two feeding siphons) that is all that you are likely to see of the living animal.

WHEN TO GO Present all year round on the lower shore. Visit on the lowest spring tides if you want to find live razor clams.

WHERE TO GO Razor clams are found on almost any

sheltered, sandy beach as long as they are always covered by the incoming tide. Look for them where the sand meets the sea. Many thousands of empty shells can be found washed up on the strandline at any time of year.

TOP TIP ★ To have any chance of finding a live razor clam, you need to creep very softly over the sand – they can sense vibrations from your footsteps.

Sand hopper

20

Sand hoppers are crustaceans, related to crabs, shrimps, barnacles and the well-known terrestrial woodlouse. They are good fun to find – and don't let the smell of rotting seaweed put you off!

The largest species is up to 2.5cm long.

LOOK FOR Almost colourless, active, shrimp-like creatures. There are many species and they are difficult to tell apart, but it is worth capturing some and looking at them closely. Different species prefer different zones on the beach. Some live in burrows, others under rocks, and some in tubes made of silt and fragments of seaweed. All help to break down washed-up seaweed and other algae and they themselves provide food for many birds, fish and crabs.

WHEN TO GO All year round, though they may be hidden deeper in the shingle or sand in winter. Some species are nocturnal, sheltering in burrows or amongst seaweed during the day, but all are fairly active and visible in the early evening.

WHERE TO GO Head for the strandline above the high water mark on any sandy or shingle beach – anywhere there is a line of rotting vegetation. Move the seaweed around to see sand hoppers of various sizes scurry away with a strange sideways gait. Also try looking under loose rocks on rocky shores.

NEWS EXTRA! After warm sunny days some species of sand hopper can be super abundant on sheltered shingle beaches, with thousands per square metre of beach. They can be seen 'jumping for joy' as they emerge from hiding.

The Great British Wildlife Hunt

15

Whelk egg case

A whelk's egg case is a classic beachcombing find along the strandline, but its unusual shape and structure can make it difficult to work out what on earth it is!

LOOK FOR Pale brown, oval, sponge-like masses, no more than 10cm long, made up of individual papery cells. They weigh virtually nothing. When freshly laid, there may have been as many as ten eggs in each cell, but usually only one hatches out and then eats all of the other eggs. Once all the eggs have hatched, the egg case, which was anchored to a rock or seaweed, breaks free and may be washed up on the beach.

Common Whelk shells. 10cm long.

WHEN TO GO Present all year. For the best beachcombing, time your visit after high spring tides or exceptionally windy weather.

WHERE TO GO Shingle and sandy beaches in all parts of the country. Look for a line of debris dumped when the last high tide receded.

TOP TIP ✱ Egg cases of the Common Whelk as large as a football are sometimes encountered – an excellent find. These are formed when several female whelks spawn at the same time and several egg cases are glued together.

The Great British Wildlife Hunt 5

Limpet

Limpets spend most of their life on the same rock, moving around to feed but nearly always returning to the same place. As they can live for 20 years, you can keep visiting the same one!

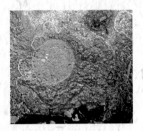

The shell can be up to 6cm long, and is often encrusted with barnacles.

LOOK FOR Nearly always seen clamped hard to rocks, frequently in groups. You can often see markings on the rocks where they have left their 'home base' to feed. Look also for depressions where limpets once lived. They either have tall, pointed shells or shorter, more flattened ones, a difference thought to be an adaptation to the different zones of the seashore.

WHEN TO GO Present all year round.

WHERE TO GO Limpets occur on all rocky shores. Look on rocks exposed at low tide, even those that are seldom underwater. They can be very obvious on the top of rocks or in rock pools and under overhangs.

Algae-encrusted rock showing the 'home scars' of Common Limpets.

NEWS EXTRA! Limpets are herbivores, feeding on both algae-encrusted rocks and young seaweed fronds. They almost always control the extent of seaweed growth on any shore, and when eradicated, as when disastrous oil spills occur, seaweeds and other algae will grow profusely in the absence of grazing.

Oil beetle

All four British oil beetles are endangered, and the top score of 50 reflects their rarity. If you find one celebrate, and then report your findings to aid their conservation!

A chunky beetle 3.5cm long, with an elongated, bloated abdomen.

BLACK OIL BEETLE

LOOK FOR Black and Violet Oil Beetles, which are difficult to tell apart, are the most likely of the four British oil beetles to be seen. An adult beetle is large, and its abdomen extends as it feeds and can look quite bloated, making the beetle unmistakable. Adults move in a very determined manner and are often spotted crossing sandy footpaths. The tiny black larvae, which have the wonderful name 'triungulins', cling to the flowers of Lesser Celandine, Buttercups and Thrift.

WHEN TO GO Adult beetles of the two commonest species are found from March to June. Warm, sunny days are best, and this is also when larvae may be found.

WHERE TO GO Flower-rich short grass, including coastal grassland, meadows and heathland, with much bare ground and sandy soil in which to lay eggs.

SCIENCE STUFF

OIL BEETLES ARE DEPENDENT ON SOLITARY BEES – THE LARVAE HITCH A RIDE WITH A BEE AND LIVE IN THE BEE'S NEST, FEEDING ON EGGS AND POLLEN. SOLITARY BEES MAKE NEST-HOLES IN SANDY BANKS WHERE THEY CAN BE FOUND LIVING SIDE BY SIDE WITH OIL BEETLES.

LARVAE OF VIOLET OIL BEETLE

The Great British Wildlife Hunt
20

Spring Squill

This captivating little flower is a relative of garden Scillas and, like these plants, can form large colonies, carpeting the clifftops and headlands in the springtime.

Up to 15cm tall, but usually much smaller due to the harsh environment they grow in.

LOOK FOR Delicate pale-blue, bell-like flowers on a thin stem, surrounded by leaves that have a distinct curl. It can be locally abundant, in some areas completely covering the ground – a wonderful sight. On sunny days it may give off a delicate scent.

WHEN TO GO In April and May to see the plants in flower. The further north you are, the later they flower.

WHERE TO GO Rocky cliff tops where there is short turf or heathy vegetation. Usually visible from coastal paths so there is no need to wander into dangerous territory near to the cliff's edge.

There may be up to 12 flowers on one stem.

SCIENCE STUFF

THERE MAY BE BLUEBELLS CLOSE BY, ALTHOUGH SELDOM IN THE SAME EXPOSED ENVIRONMENTS. BLUEBELLS ARE ALWAYS TALLER, WITH HANGING, DARKER BLUE BELLS.

The Great British Wildlife Hunt

25

Little Tern

Terns were once called 'sea swallows' because of their forked tails and fast, graceful flight. This is the daintiest and really lives up to its name, being the smallest British tern.

LOOK FOR A small tern with a disproportionately large head and fast, jerky, wing beats. Little Terns hover, peering intently into the water before plunging to catch a fish, often several times in succession, and demand attention with their high-pitched, squeaky calls. The summer plumage, with a white forehead and yellow bill, is unique. By the autumn, however, the bill may be an undistinguished black (and all terns have a white forehead in autumn). Look for the elaborate breeding display, and once the young have fledged watch the young birds practise diving for fish – they take a while to learn this skill.

WHEN TO GO A summer visitor, arriving in April and May and leaving by August or September. Spends the winter in West Africa.

COMMON TERN

WHERE TO GO Breeds in loose colonies on sand or shingle beaches. Can be seen feeding in the sea close to these areas and around nearby estuaries. Find a comfortable spot beside their colonies, take your binoculars and watch their behaviour.

SANDWICH TERN

NEWS EXTRA! Little Terns prefer to nest on rocky shores and shingle beaches. Because the eggs are so well camouflaged and the birds are sensitive to disturbance, these colonies are usually protected.

The Great British Wildlife Hunt

25

Squat Lobster

You will be greedy for more than a glimpse of a Squat Lobster; its personality shines out even from the dark crevices where it makes its home.

An adult's visible body size is about 3.5cm. The tail is held under the body creating the 'squat' appearance.

LOOK FOR Long front claws, held loosely, poking out from under a rock. Look for a rapid, torpedo-like movement, backwards or sideways, when you move a rock – it is likely to be a Squat Lobster trying to remain in its hiding place. The long claws on the three pairs of walking legs help it cling to its rock crevice in rough weather. Handle it carefully – the front pincers can nip – and put it back where you found it.

WHEN TO GO Present all year round. From April to June it may be small, but are easier to catch. By mid-summer all are able to move very quickly. They breed in the winter months and that is also a good time to spot them.

WHERE TO GO The lower shore when rocks are exposed at low tide. Search in the deeper rock pools near to the sea's edge, lifting loose rocks carefully. Squat Lobsters particularly like small crevices (look with a torch) and share their pools with tiny fish, shrimps and prawns.

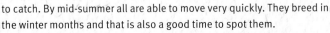

NEWS EXTRA! Squat Lobsters are master at escaping, being surprisingly fast and well camouflaged. When threatened, they will also flap their tails wildly in an attempt to distract you, so divers often call them 'flappers'.

The Great British Wildlife Hunt

35

Pipefish

Related to sea horses and sea dragons, pipefish have a similar 'nose', but are more snake-like (don't worry – they are harmless). You will have to be eagle-eyed to spot one.

LOOK FOR Long, tubular fish with slightly thicker heads and long snouts. They are well camouflaged and poor swimmers, often remaining very still, making them hard to spot – watch carefully for their tiny movements. The commonest is the Worm Pipefish, which looks like a piece of leather bootlace and is up to 15cm long. The largest, the Greater Pipefish, can be almost 50cm long – a hugely exciting find. It can hold itself upright, just like a sea horse, amongst the seaweed.

WHEN TO GO Pipefish can be seen all year. Use a tide table to find the dates and times of the lowest tides and follow the tide out. They may also be found washed up on the beach after winter storms. There are often 'good' years, after which they are not seen again for a while.

WHERE TO GO Rock pools. Head for sheltered spots and pools with plenty of seaweed and shallow water near the sea's edge. The larger species can be found amongst seaweeds, the smaller ones amongst the rocks too.

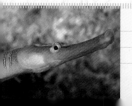

TOP TIP ✷ Look closely at their eyes: they move independently, like a chameleon. In pipefish it is the males that brood the eggs in a pouch until they hatch out.

Shore Crab

Often the first crabs to be found at the beach, they are beloved of children with nets or lines. All crabs have five pairs of legs, the front pair being the 'pincers', specialised for grabbing prey.

Colour and pattern are variable.

LOOK FOR Rock pools where bubbles beneath the sand give them away, as do patterns in the mud suggesting the sideways movements of the crabs. The shells are wider than they are long, no bigger than 6cm deep and 9cm wide, and, although often called Green Shore Crabs, they can be various colours and have different patterns on the shell. A crab with red eyes and flattened, paddle-like back legs is the otherwise similarly coloured Velvet Swimming Crab.

WHEN TO GO May to October, on any low tide. This is when the crabs are resting – they do most of their feeding at high tide, and often at night. In winter, they head for deeper water.

WHERE TO GO Common in a wide variety of habitats, both natural and man-made, from saltmarsh pools and estuaries to rock pools and the nooks and crannies close to breakwaters on sandy beaches. Look under seaweed and in rock crevices but be quick as crabs can rapidly disappear from view, digging into the sand or squeezing into small crevices.

TOP TIP ✳ Join others with a line and some bacon pieces to catch Shore Crabs at jetties and harbours around the country. Pick up your crab from the top, holding it at the broadest point of the shell; then, with its pincers underneath, it cannot possibly nip. Do follow the 'crab-catchers code' and put your crabs back in the water gently.

The Great British Wildlife Hunt

20

Wall Brown

Once a common butterfly in parks and gardens, this species has declined massively and any sightings should definitely be passed on to the local butterfly recorder.

Wingspan 4.5-5cm. Males and females have a similar pattern, but the female is usually paler, making the eyespots more prominent.

The caterpillar feeds on various grasses and is hard to spot.

LOOK FOR One of the brighter 'brown' butterflies, often found sunning itself on bare patches of ground, or on walls and rocks. Flies up when disturbed, only to settle a few yards away on another sunny, bare patch. Wall Browns are well camouflaged against these bare surfaces when their wings are closed. Adults take nectar from flowers, particular favourites being Water Mint, hawkweeds and Marjoram.

WHEN TO GO Sunny days. There are two generations a year, with adults flying from early May to late June and again from late July into September.

WHERE TO GO Coastal footpaths where there is some bare ground, vegetated shingle banks, sand dunes and cliff tops. This butterfly has undergone a steep decline in numbers recently, and it is now rare at inland sites.

TOP TIP ★ Egg-laying occurs on sandy banks where the food plants grow. The areas around rabbit holes are good places to look for egg-laying females.

Thrift

15

A characteristic seaside plant, the bobbing flowers of Thrift are never far away in most coastal habitats. It is a beautiful but tough flower that can cope with the harshest conditions.

Flowering stem up to 30cm tall but can be much shorter than this.

LOOK FOR Small leaves in dense, rounded cushions, with several wiry, leafless stems carrying clusters of pink, tufted flowers. Thrift usually grows with a great variety of other flowers such as Kidney Vetch, plantains, Wild Thyme and Bird's-foot Trefoil.

WHEN TO GO Some plants can be in flower from April to October, but for the best displays go in May or June. The papery bracts persist all through the year.

WHERE TO GO You will find it flowering in saltmarshes, on rocky or sandy coastal cliffs, in cliff top grassland, on shingle, and even on walls by the sea. It can look especially spectacular on Cornish ledges in the springtime.

BIRD'S-FOOT TREFOIL

TOP TIP ✷ The flowers are visited by many insects, including some beautiful day-flying moths, such as the Six-spot Burnet (p.179).

Dark Green Fritillary

All large butterflies are arresting and this one is no exception – it can appear most unexpectedly – and is a real stunner when on the wing.

Wingspan 55–60cm.

LOOK FOR A large, strong-flying butterfly, bright orange with darker markings. Fritillaries are often difficult to identify, so when stationary with the wings closed – check for the green colouring at the base of the hind wing. It is the most widespread of all the fritillaries.

WHEN TO GO Adults fly from June in the south, to August in the north. Sunny days are best, although some cloud may mean they sit around basking for longer. In April and May, look for spiky black caterpillars feeding on the leaves of violets.

UNDERSIDE OF WING

WHERE TO GO Although not strictly a coastal species, you should find it wherever there are flowery grasslands. Ungrazed coastal cliff tops, dunes, and vegetated shingle banks are good habitats. Groups of trees and hedgerows near the coast provide some shelter, and it often flies up when you walk by.

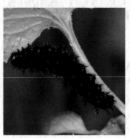

CATERPILLAR

TOP TIP ★ Dark Green Fritillaries like to feed on the flowers of thistles and knapweeds, so staking out a good stand of these may be rewarding.

The Great British Wildlife Hunt
20

Yellow Horned Poppy

A wonderful British native that bears large yellow flowers. Easy to identify and an unforgettable sight when en masse and in full flower on a shingle bank.

Typically 50cm tall, but can be larger.

The plant is named after the curved seedpods.

LOOK FOR A robust plant with many stems arising from one centre point, making it appear rather bushy. The leaves are blue-green with stiff hairs and the large golden-yellow flowers are obvious. The many black seeds are formed in long, thin, curved, pods, the 'horns', which are just as obvious as the flowers. They split down the middle, dispersing the seeds over the shingle, and then turn black for the winter.

WHEN TO GO The best flowering times are June and July, but you will find flowers on the plants until September.

WHERE TO GO Shingle banks close to the sea. The plants can be common, forming extensive patches and sometimes almost covering the surface of the bank.

Flowers 6–9cm across.

TOP TIP ★ The tough, evergreen leaves of young, non-flowering plants hug the pebbles in an attractive rosette.

The Great British Wildlife Hunt
15

Sea Bindweed

Sea Bindweed may be overlooked, but it is very pretty, whether winding its way amongst other plants or in solitary clumps.

LOOK FOR Beautiful trumpet-shaped flowers, striped like a stick of rock. Much like the weed of gardens and fields, but this bindweed is never a climber, it always hugs the ground. The leaves are kidney-shaped and rather fleshy – they are readily eaten by Rabbits.

Flowers up to 4cm across.

WHEN TO GO The main flowering period is June to August, but you may find it in flower up to October.

WHERE TO GO Sand dunes, sandy beaches and the edges of paths in sandy grassland by the sea.

TOP TIP ✳ May be confused with Field Bindweed (left) which can also have pink and white striped blooms, but Field Bindweed has smaller flowers and thinner leaves that are more arrow-shaped and not so fleshy; Field Bindweed can also climb.

The Great British Wildlife Hunt

10

Six-spot Burnet Moth

These day-flying moths contain the poison cyanide in their bodies and alert potential predators with their bright warning colours. Not a moth to be trifled with.

Wingspan 3–3.8cm.

LOOK FOR The flitting flight of this moth and its black and red colouring. There can be many flying in one small area. Confident in their poisoners' guise, mating pairs on grass stems are very visible. In fact, the eggs and caterpillars are also conspicuous on the food plant as these too are laden with cyanide to make them unpalatable. Look also for the straw-coloured papery cocoons, actually spun from silk, and very tough. Although very visible when attached to wiry grass stems, they are safe from predatory birds. Often the adult moth can be seen emerging, leaving its black pupal case protruding from the cocoon.

WHEN TO GO Adults are on the wing from June to August, and sunny days are best. The caterpillars can be seen in April and May.

WHERE TO GO Flower-filled coastal grassland, cliff tops and sand dunes, where the caterpillars' food plant, Bird's-foot Trefoil, grows.

SCIENCE STUFF

THESE MOTHS ALSO USE CYANIDE IN COURTSHIP. THE FEMALE GIVES OFF A PLUME OF HYDROGEN CYANIDE GAS TO ATTRACT THE MALES. THE MALES GIVE THE FEMALES A LITTLE PARCEL OF CYANIDE TOO, AND THIS LITTLE EXTRA HELPS THE FEMALES TO PROTECT THE EGGS.

The Great British Wildlife Hunt 10

Marsh samphire

A familiarity with this strange plant is essential for lovers of wild food: it is succulent and tastes of the sea, not surprising as it is often washed by the tides twice a day.

A sturdy, upright plant, that grows up to 18cm tall.

LOOK FOR Growing en masse, samphire can form lawn-like expanses of upright, fresh green shoots. The fleshy plants resemble a cactus without the spines and have a tree-like growth pattern. By late August they turn red and yellow at the tips and even later in the year bathe the saltmarshes in rich gold and purple, a great subject for photography.

WHEN TO GO Samphire is an annual plant and begins its growth when the weather warms up in June. By October, it has gone to seed and the stems are washed away by the tides.

WHERE TO GO Grows on the mud of saltmarshes and estuaries, with different species occurring in different zones. It can also be found in wet, saline areas and seepages behind sea walls and shingle banks.

TOP TIP ★ A popular foraging food now found in some supermarkets! If collecting for eating, cut off the stems with scissors rather than pulling up the whole plant so that it can grow again and pick only in areas covered by the sea every day.

The Great British Wildlife Hunt
10

Sea Lavender

One of our most spectacular wild flowers, painting the saltmarshes lavender-blue when in flower. Not related to Lavender, the name comes from the colour of the flowers.

Flower stems to 40cm high.

LOOK FOR The tough wiry stems and lavender blue petals are distinctive. The pale, chaffy sepals surrounding the flowers persist well after the petals have fallen and are characteristic of this plant.

WHEN TO GO Plants can be in flower from June to October, but the main period is July to August.

WHERE TO GO Saltmarshes, saline pools and seepages behind sea walls and shingle banks. A similar but smaller and daintier plant, Rock Sea Lavender, is found on rocky cliffs on the south and west coasts as well as on the drier upper saltmarsh.

TOP TIP ✳ The presence of bee hives on the saltmarsh is a sure sign of locally abundant stands of Sea Lavender. The flowers produce copious amounts of nectar, resulting in a sought-after honey.

The Great British Wildlife Hunt
20

Sea Holly

An unmistakable seashore plant, architectural in appearance. The rather statuesque flowers are often surrounded by insects.

Flowers can be up to 60cm high.

LOOK FOR Tough, blue-grey leaves on rigid stems mean that individual plants stand out amongst the surrounding vegetation. It is not related to Holly, but lives up to its name with very prickly, very Holly-like leaves. The leaf edges have long, tough spines

– a great defence against grazing animals of all sizes. A ruff of spiny leaves or bracts sits below the flowers, making them very attractive.

WHEN TO GO Flowering from July to September, it is a genuine seaside holiday plant.

WHERE TO GO Sea Holly will grow on the relatively loose sand of young sand dunes and may spread onto nearby sandy shingle.

NEWS EXTRA! Despite all its prickles, Sea Holly is a sweet plant. Burnet Moths devour its nectar and the roots were once dug up, candied, and eaten as sweets.

The Great British Wildlife Hunt

20

Wader roost

In autumn and winter there is no finer site than thousands of wading birds flying in and jostling for position as they roost on the higher ground at high tide.

Notice how species group together – these are Oystercatchers and Knots.

LOOK FOR Large flocks of different waders all bunched together: Dunlins, Knots, Oystercatchers, Bar-tailed Godwits, Redshanks, Ringed Plovers, Grey Plovers, Sanderlings and Curlews. Stop about 300 metres away from the birds to avoid disturbing them.

WHEN TO GO August to March, when the numbers of birds are boosted by winter visitors. Any exceptionally high tide at other times of the year will find resident birds roosting on any ground that is not underwater.

WHERE TO GO Waders feed on estuaries and mudflats, roosting on adjacent higher ground, usually on saltmarshes, sand bars and sea walls. On the highest 'spring' tides of the autumn, however, the whole marsh may be flooded and the birds forced onto fields and pools just inland of the sea wall. Coastal bird reserves may organise events on these very highest tides, or find your own spot.

TOP TIP ★ You will need binoculars or a telescope to see individual species but much of the spectacle involves the birds in the air. Take a chair, sit back and watch.

OPEN COUNTRYSIDE

Included in this section are the areas of the countryside where humans live and work and have done for thousands of years, creating the familiar landscapes we see today. It includes farmland, with associated hedgerows, green lanes and copses; towns and villages with commons, churchyards and old railway lines; and even cities with their parks, waste ground and old industrial sites.

Wildlife has had to adapt to this man-made landscape and over the centuries there have been winners and losers: Brown Bears, Beavers and Wolves were lost a long time ago. Since the1940s, there has been a second agricultural revolution, resulting in larger fields and achieving high yields. As a consequence habitat for wildlife has shrunk dramatically, and is still shrinking. Most of the countryside is still a mosaic of fields and hedgerows, but we now have to look much harder to find places that have escaped 'improvement' and are rich in wildlife. However, do keep walking in the countryside: there are still special places to be discovered, while recording the wildlife you find will provide great benefits to conservation.

The farmed countryside

Farmers are responsible for managing around 75 per cent of the UK's land. In Britain the climate and landscape lends itself to two distinct types of farming. In areas of higher rainfall, especially the hills of the north and west, grassland has dominated, with cattle and sheep farming. In the drier lowlands, especially in the south and east, arable crops are grown, the land ploughed to grow wheat, barley, root crops, beans and peas. Most modern farming is intensive, with high inputs of fertilisers and pesticides, and is distinctly wildlife un-friendly.

However some crops are of value to wildlife. Oil-seed rape and clovers provide nectar for bees, while brassicas (the cabbage family) are good for Large and Small White butterflies. Sugar beet and stubble fields when left un-ploughed provide a home for many arable weeds. There are also many schemes in which farmers receive payments to help them to benefit wildlife in all sorts of ways. Mostly these involve setting aside part of a field for wildlife as a 'conservation headland', to create flower-rich margins – areas left un-sprayed or even sown with flowers to encourage a range of arable weeds and beneficial insects.

Farmers also maintain most of the features that make the British countryside so special: hedges, green lanes, ditches, woods and copses all help to increase the wildlife diversity in the farmed landscape. Farmland can be explored via footpaths and

bridleways, or on permitted paths, and you should find poppies (p.208), Brown Hares (p.190) and butterflies. It is well worth visiting on 'farm open days' to get an insight into how farms work.

Grassland

Grasslands cover around 35 per cent of the countryside and come in many different guises. The poorest for wildlife are those that are 'improved': regularly ploughed, seeded with coarse grasses and heavily fertilised. Sadly, most pastures are now 'improved' and a field full of cattle or sheep may have very little to offer the wildlife enthusiast, nor do most fields cut for hay, silage or haylage.

The best grasslands for wildlife have been undisturbed for tens and even hundreds of years, have not been ploughed or seeded and are low in nutrients, producing some of the loveliest habitats for wild flowers and insects that you will find. On dry soils over chalk and limestone look for Common Spotted Orchids, Cowslips and Marbled White butterflies (pp.207, 198, 211). On wetter soils meadows and pastures are equally rich, and often attract Barn Owls (p.196), while in the uplands acid grassland and hay meadows are home to Heath Spotted Orchid (p. 77).

Many of these habitat types have been covered elsewhere in this book. These flower-rich grasslands are not natural, but are the direct result of traditional farming practices. These 'unimproved' flower-rich grasslands were once found in every parish in the country, but are now reduced to scattered fragments and make up less than three per cent of Britain's grassland. Most of the remaining large areas of wildlife-rich grassland survive in nature reserves; otherwise you will have to look for road verges, churchyards and the small, isolated fields and other pockets of good habitat on farms where the old traditions are maintained.

Green lanes, hedgerows, roadside trees and verges

Britain has thousands of miles of roads, most of which are bordered with hedgerows, while the mosaic of fields is also divided up by hedges in many places. Hedgerows vary tremendously in their value to wildlife, depending on their history and how they are managed. Some planted hedges are dominated by hawthorns, but others, especially older hedges, have a great variety of trees and shrubs, including Blackthorn, wild roses, Hazel and Field Maple, all excellent caterpillar food plants. Look for hedges that are not cut until late winter, or are lightly trimmed – these will have berries and nuts for birds. Many hedges have trees as well as shrubs and older trees especially may be full of wildlife surprises.

Between the hedge and the road there is usually a grassy verge. These can create a refuge for grassland plants and animals, although many are now far too rich in nitrogenous fertilisers (from the adjacent fields and from car exhausts) and are dominated by coarse grasses and plants that enjoy lots of nutrients such as Stinging Nettles and Hogweed; nevertheless, they can be good places to look for insects. The best verges tend to be on light, sandy or chalky soils, or on steep slopes, and the very best are often 'Roadside Nature Reserves' – look for the little posts that mark these gems. It is also worth seeking out Green Lanes, broad grassy tracks (often a public footpath or bridleway) bordered by hedges. These were once used to move cattle and sheep, and are now potential havens for wildlife. And, wherever they are, most hedgerows, apart from the most badly managed, provide important corridors for wildlife to move between one habitat and another.

Commons

Commons are areas of land where some of the local population have (or had) 'common rights', usually rights to graze animals and collect firewood etc. These rights often came with a house, and could be bought and sold. (Contrary to popular myth, a common is not necessarily in 'common' ownership, and there was no automatic right of access until the 2000 Countryside and Rights of Way Act.) Due to their complex ownership, commons often have a great sense of local history and the piecemeal management often results in a mosaic of mini-habitats, from copses and clearings to grassland and ponds that support a wide range of plants and animals. If you are lucky enough to have a common close to home it is well worth making it a regular 'patch'.

Old railway lines

Up and down the country former railway lines have been turned into footpaths and cycle routes and these can be great places to go to find wildlife. On the steep embankments there is often short, sparse grassland and scrub, open but sheltered, just the sort of conditions that attract many plants, insects and birds.

Landscaped gardens and parkland

Whether old country estates, suburban splendours or urban open spaces, these gardens attract millions of people each year. All have some great landscapes, often with fantastic specimen trees, wide, open spaces with herds of deer, small woods and lakes and flower-filled formal gardens. Despite the formality, they can often be excellent for wildlife. Look for the quieter footpaths and sheltered places to seek out some of the shyer species, such as Little Owl (p.191) and Green Woodpecker (p.194).

Country parks

Mostly close to towns and cities, and with good access and visitor facilities, country parks can be excellent places to introduce yourself to lots of wildlife. Some are real 'hotspots' for wildlife, with a variety of sensitively managed habitats. In others, the habitats are not so special, and the large numbers of visitors create significant disturbance and you are unlikely to come across the more specialist plants and insects that are found in 'wilder' habitats.

Churchyards

Quiet oases in urban areas or pockets of calm in the countryside, all are worth exploring. Spring can be an especially good time, with birds in the surrounding trees and flowers covering the ground. Some churchyards are now managed with conservation in mind, with areas left for the grass to grow long for part of the year. These can be full of flowers, support insects and small mammals, and be hunting grounds for owls. Some of the largest and old Yew trees can be found in churchyards; look for Redwings and Fieldfares (p.000) eating the berries in winter.

Old industrial sites

Many old industrial sites have been landscaped and converted into green spaces. They are sometimes superb places to find wildlife, close to, or even within, towns and cities. The type of soil varies greatly – waste from mining operations or chemical works may have been dumped on the land, creating challenging conditions that support specialist plants and animals, such as brilliant displays of marsh orchids and Bee Orchids (p.113 and p.203).

Quarries and gravel pits

Abandoned sand pits and quarries, especially on limestone and chalk, may be of great age, with grass-covered 'hills and holes' providing warm, sheltered south-facing slopes, great for wild flowers and insects, while trees and shrubs provide habitat for birds.

Flooded gravel workings and brick pits dug into clay are often great habitats for many water birds and often have facilities for bird watching and walking. Indeed, some of the largest developments now only go ahead on the condition that they are turned over to wildlife once work has finished.

Waste ground

Areas in and around towns and cities where housing or industrial units have been demolished or abandoned are often unique in having little soil and many patches of bare ground. Whether large or small, these are ideal places for plants to colonise and you will find many 'weedy' species such as buddleias, willowherbs, thistles, ragworts and poppies (see p.208), as well as a variety of 'garden escapes'. With so many sources of nectar and many larval food plants, they become great places to look for butterflies and day-flying moths. Always check that these sites have public access.

The Great British Wildlife Hunt

15

Brown Hare

Built for speed with strong legs and excellent eyesight and hearing, the Brown Hare is well equipped to move out of danger.

The black tips to the ears are noticeable at a distance.

LOOK FOR Much larger than a Rabbit, with longer legs and longer, black-tipped ears. The colour of their fur remains the same all year round and males and females are difficult to tell apart. You will often see a lone Brown Hare racing across open fields or hopping slowly along a country lane. Early on spring mornings, however, find one of their favourite spots and you may see two of them 'boxing'. It may be a female warning off an unwanted male or two males fighting.

WHEN TO GO Present all year, but easiest to see from September to April when crops are still low. Early morning and late afternoon are the most rewarding times of day.

WHERE TO GO Large arable fields, grassland or downland, often with hedges and scattered woodland. Watch from green lanes, footpaths and quiet country roads.

TOP TIP ★ Hares can be very shy. They rest during the day and are well hidden when crouching low on the ground, but you may startle one unexpectedly out of the long grass.

Little Owl

Living up to its name, this owl is small and very cute. It was introduced to Britain from Europe in the 19th century and is now fairly widespread in open countryside.

Length 22cm. The size of a Starling but much dumpier.

LOOK FOR A chunky, flat-headed owl with a fierce expression, usually perched on a telegraph pole, fence post, large tree or rocky outcrop. It will bob from side to side if disturbed and its silhouette as the light fades is characteristic. Little Owls can be very vocal, with the commonest call a cat-like *meiow*.

WHEN TO GO Present all year and active in daylight, they are best looked for in the early morning and evening.

WHERE TO GO Anywhere with suitable holes for nest sites: parkland, farmland and riverside meadows with old trees; they will even nest in derelict buildings and walls, often using the same site each year.

NEWS EXTRA! Spice up a rural car journey with a 'Spot the Little Owl' game. Once you know the sort of place to look, you may be lucky ...

Flight fast and undulating.

A typical nesting tree.

Often perches on an isolated post.

The Great British Wildlife Hunt

30

Stoat

Although it mostly goes about its business unseen, some great wildlife moments can nevertheless be had with this cheeky mammal, which will even venture into gardens.

The black tip to the tail distinguishes a Stoat from a Weasel as does its larger size.

LOOK FOR The fast-moving Stoat is most often seen dashing across a road. It runs very fast, with leaps and bounds, often stopping to scan around, standing on its hind legs. If you see a Stoat running off, watch where it disappears to and sit downwind to wait; there is every chance that the Stoat's natural curiosity will make it reappear and take a look at you.

WHEN TO GO Present all year round. Stoats are active by day and night. Groups of females are sometimes seen from June onwards, hunting together with their young.

WHERE TO GO Places with lots of Rabbits, which are their favourite prey; they sometimes make their dens in old Rabbit burrows. Farmland with plenty of scrub, hedgerows, hollow trees and walls (they like to hunt along walls), young woodland, and Stoats will even enter large gardens and parks looking for prey.

TOP TIP ★ In cold winters the Stoat's coat turns white, sometimes even in lowland Britain. Score ten extra for seeing a Stoat in 'ermine'.

Skylark

Although famously celebrated by authors and poets, not everyone knows the song of a Skylark. Make sure you visit open countryside to listen to its wonderful, evocative song from high above.

Length 18cm. The short crest can be obvious, but not always.

Similar to a Meadow Pipit but the latter is a slighter bird with a thinner bill and squeaky call.

LOOK FOR A pale brown bird, larger than a sparrow, mottled and streaked dark brown, with a paler throat and belly, pink legs and short crest. In flight look for white outer tail feathers and a narrow white trailing edge to the wing, and listen for the mellow *chirrup* call. The Skylark's song flight is the sight and sound of summer. It hangs almost motionless in the air, nearly too high to see, producing an apparently endless, pleasant, liquid warbling, before eventually plummeting swiftly to the ground.

WHEN TO GO Present all year, with the song most likely to be heard from March onwards.

WHERE TO GO Skylarks like an open vista where they can see for a good distance all around. Listen for their song in grassy and arable fields, on open heaths and moors, coastal dunes, cliff-top grassland and downland. In winter they can form quite large flocks, roaming around fields and other open ground, and they are often found on saltmarshes.

NEWS EXTRA! The number of breeding Skylarks has been declining for many years, largely due to changing farming practices. Farmers are now being encouraged to help by leaving patches of bare ground in their autumn-sown cereals for Skylarks to feed and nest in.

The Great British Wildlife Hunt
25

Green Woodpecker

The largest British woodpecker, once known as the 'yaffle'; its fantastic call sounds like manic laughter as it echoes across fields and commons.

Length 32cm. Usually seen on the ground or flying off, calling loudly.

LOOK FOR Jackdaw-sized, with green upperparts, a black face and red crown, and yellow rump that is conspicuous in flight; its distinctive colouring makes identification easy. So does the magical call – a rapid series of 10 to 20 loud notes: *kle-kle-kle* … Green Woodpeckers nearly always feed on the ground, largely on ants and their pupae, and will spend much time probing into short meadow turf and ant hills, often spending some time at one spot. They also hop for short distances following ant trails in the grass.

WHEN TO GO Present all year round, rarely moving far from breeding areas. Both parents feed the young for up to seven weeks after they fledge so family groups may be obvious in midsummer. In winter, although they are more solitary, Green Woodpeckers may roost together in an old nest hole.

WHERE TO GO Unimproved, short grassland where there are lots of ants – ant hills are a good clue. Also try orchards, old parkland and formal gardens with large, old lawns. They nest in holes in mature trees.

SCIENCE STUFF

THE GREEN WOODPECKER HAS A VERY LONG TONGUE. THE TIP IS EXTREMELY MOBILE AND HAS GLANDS THAT PRODUCE STICKY SALIVA, ADAPTED FOR PICKING UP ANTS.

Red Fox

Needing no introduction, you either love or hate them. It requires skill to find a country fox, unlike the bold urban fox, which may happily set up home in your garden.

Fox poo.

LOOK FOR You are most likely to encounter a country fox if you find its den. Look for enlarged Rabbit burrows: foxholes often have food debris around them, with paths leading to and fro. Look around for their tracks – much like a dog's, but when trotting they travel in a straight line – and for other signs: fox poo is often left on top of grassy tussocks. Their calls can be heard in mid-winter: high-pitched screeches and a series of bark-like *wow-wows*. In comparison, urban foxes are much easier to see as they are quite happy in city streets, eating discarded food as well as rats and mice, and using quiet gardens to hide in the daytime.

WHEN TO GO In May and June cubs will be playing around the den and the adults coming and going with food. Watch at dawn and dusk if you can, and from a distance – the female won't come near if she can smell you! Outside this period their whereabouts can be unpredictable.

WHERE TO GO Woodland edges and clearings and fields with Rabbit holes. Foxes roam widely when hunting – use binoculars to spot them.

TOP TIP ★ Learn to recognise the rather pungent smell the male fox uses to mark his territory. Even urban foxes can sometimes be elusive, but a remote 'camera trap' can still produce great shots.

Barn Owl

Hauntingly beautiful, this 'white' owl with a heart-shaped face is uncommon in many parts of Britain and you may have to travel in order to see one.

Length 34cm, smaller than a Tawny Owl.

Large head and broad wings.

LOOK FOR Barn Owls nearly always look very pale in flight, even though their upperparts are actually a mixture of gold and grey. Watch them hunting over long grass, looking from side to side and occasionally dropping down and disappearing into the grass. If successful, they will emerge and fly off carrying a vole or mouse in their claws. Barn Owls regularly perch in the open on fence posts and dead trees, when their white face and underparts and upright shape is distinctive.

WHEN TO GO Present all year, rarely moving far from breeding areas. Mostly a nocturnal hunter, but often seen in the early morning and evening, and even during the day in winter and when feeding young.

WHERE TO GO Farmland with a mixture of rough grassland and scrub, woodland, wide hedgerows and grassy road verges, also often seen on coastal marshes – all places with Short-tailed Field Voles, the Barn Owl's favourite prey.

TOP TIP ✴ The distribution of the Barn Owl may be limited by the availability of suitable nest sites, particularly barns and old trees. To make up for this Barn Owl boxes are commonly erected in good areas. If you see an owl, watch from a distance with binoculars to avoid disturbing it.

Hedgehog

The only British mammal to have spines, it is surprisingly difficult to spot away from gardens, probably due to its nocturnal habits.

Adults can be quite large, up to 30cm long.

LOOK FOR Hedgehogs are almost always nocturnal so look for them at night with a torch. Their noisy foraging habits give them away; listen for their snuffling – once heard, never forgotten! Hedgehogs may travel 1 to 2km per night across all sorts of terrain in their search for food. One of the greatest threats to them is traffic, and many are killed on the roads each year. Often the most obvious sign that hedgehogs are in the area is the presence of their characteristic poo – black, shiny and full of beetle wing cases.

WHEN TO GO Present all year but Hedgehogs hibernate under hedges, in the roots of trees, in piles of brushwood, in Rabbit burrows, sheds and compost heaps in cold weather from November onwards, waking up again in March. The young are born from May to July, occasionally later.

WHERE TO GO Dry, grassy places. As well as in gardens, look for them in farmland with plenty of cover, commons and woodlands.

NEWS EXTRA! Hedgehog numbers have declined by as much as 25 per cent in many areas of Britain in the last ten years. Many of those taken to Hedgehog rescue centres have been poisoned, a good reason not to use slug pellets or other poisons. Make your garden hedgehog friendly: don't be too tidy, ban pesticides and provide them with a safe place to nest and overwinter. Help with surveys too, by recording any sightings.

The Great British Wildlife Hunt

15

Cowslip

One of the earliest meadow plants to flower in spring, with thousands growing together in some special places, a sight that is sadly all too rare nowadays.

LOOK FOR Cluster of up to 30 subtly scented, small yellow flowers with orange spots in the centre, all hanging to one side of the upright stem. A little like a Primrose and sometimes flowering together, but the Primrose has larger flowers, with only one per stem. Depending on the site, Cowslips can vary considerably in stature – very short with few flowers on poor, heavily grazed chalky soils, much taller and more robust in damper meadows.

WHEN TO GO Flowers in April and May. The seedheads are obvious for a while if the grass is not grazed or cut for hay.

WHERE TO GO Commonest on chalk and limestone soils, including unimproved meadows and road verges (and often planted along main roads). The presence of Cowslips usually indicates a good area for wildflowers and it is worth returning to botanise later in the year.

NEWS EXTRA! There are many references in old herbals to the uses of Cowslips: the petals for Cowslip wine and in salads and the leaves and roots for ointments, while entire flower heads were made into decorative Cowslip 'balls'.

Holly Blue

One of the first butterflies of the year, this is the easiest of the blue butterflies to identify and the one most likely to be seen in gardens.

Wingspan 30mm.

Females usually have a broader black band around the border, but they rarely open their wings

LOOK FOR A small blue butterfly that usually sits with its wings closed showing the silvery-blue underside of the wings. It is commonly found resting or fluttering around the caterpillars' two food plants: Holly in the spring, Ivy for the second generation. The adults prefer honeydew and plant sap to nectar, but may be attracted down to flower-rich verges and garden borders and can be seen on the ground around puddles, damp mud and animal waste.

WHEN TO GO Look for the adults on sunny spring days from early April to mid June, with a second brood in southern counties from mid-July to early September.

WHERE TO GO Widespread in many habitats including hedgerows, green lanes, field edges and woodland rides and glades, and may be common in parks, gardens and churchyards. Unlike many of the blues, the Holly Blue does not form colonies, although several may be seen together around Ivy and Holly bushes.

TOP TIP ✳ Often flies high around bushes and shrubs and can be recognised by this behaviour alone.

The Great British Wildlife Hunt

25

Cuckoo

A real harbinger of spring after our long, grey winters, the Cuckoo is unfortunately fast becoming a rare sight (and sound) in much of the countryside.

Length 33cm, with long pointed wings and a long tail.

LOOK FOR The double-noted *cuck-coo* call is unmistakable, but is only given by the male in spring and early summer. Males and females look similar: learn to recognise their shape, which makes it easier to spot them when they are perched in the open. In flight, Cuckoos are rather hawk-like. Small birds sometimes fly up and mob them, perhaps because of their resemblance to a bird of prey, but equally likely because they recognise them as Cuckoos and know they are a potential threat to their nests.

WHEN TO GO A summer visitor, Cuckoos arrive in mid April. The adult birds leave by early July, but the juveniles, raised by another species of bird, are left to find their own way to Africa around late August.

WHERE TO GO Farmland, especially areas with tall hedges, commons and unimproved grassland. Also wetlands, reedbeds, heathland, and moorland.

TOP TIP ✱ The female Cuckoo lays eggs in the nests of other birds including Meadow Pipits, Dunnocks and Reed Warblers. She flies around her chosen territory watching for her host birds nest-building and homes in when their egg-laying is completed to lay a single egg in each nest of the right host that she finds.

Young cuckoo and Dunnock 'mother'.

Sweet Briar

Wild roses can be difficult to identify but on a warm day in early June the spicy apple scent of the Sweet Briar rose fills the air and it is easily found and identified.

Dark pink flowers 3–4cm across stand out from the rich green of the foliage.

LOOK FOR An upright, freestanding shrub rose, either an isolated shrub or part of a hedgerow. Sweet Briars begin to flower earlier than all other roses except the Burnet Rose but that species usually has almost white flowers, many tiny leaves and is a low-growing, suckering plant. The rather commoner Dog Rose is scrambling, with long arching stems. It often has white flowers and is never apple-scented.

WHEN TO GO Flowers in June and July, with bright red fruits to follow (the 'hips'). The scent can be particularly strong on warm, rainy days.

WHERE TO GO Open scrub, hedgerows, green lanes, woodland edges and commons, especially on chalky soils.

SCIENCE STUFF

THE GLORIOUS SMELL COMES FROM THE STICKY, APPLE-SCENTED HAIRS ON THE UNDERSIDE OF THE LEAVES, LEAF STALKS AND, MOST NOTICEABLY, THE FLOWER STALKS. THESE HAIRS, TOGETHER WITH THE SCENTED FLOWERS, LADEN WITH NECTAR, HELP TO ATTRACT INSECTS THAT, IN TURN, POLLINATE THE PLANTS.

The Great British Wildlife Hunt
20

Silver Y Moth

This day-flying moth is a summer visitor to Britain and is usually abundant, sometimes spectacularly so. It is always busy, feeding while beating its wings

The 'Y' mark on the wing is always present.

LOOK FOR A fast-flying moth, its rapid wing-beats can appear a bit of a blur. Several may gather around the same plant, hovering in front of the flowers and each using their long proboscis to extract nectar.

WHEN TO GO May to September, even later in mild weather. Silver Ys are mostly active from late afternoon onwards, well before other moths, but can be seen at almost any time of day.

WHERE TO GO Almost any grassy place with flowers to provide nectar. An immigrant from Europe, numbers vary from year to year and those that arrive in the spring may breed here. Usually common visitors to gardens, but in years when they are scarce, head for coastal grasslands in the late summer if you haven't seen one yet in your garden.

TOP TIP ✳ Readily disturbed from the vegetation on dull days, but also attracted to lights at night – a moth trap is a really great investment.

Bee Orchid

Wow! An unexpectedly exotic flower springing up from nowhere on your local patch. The colour, the shape, the size – this plant definitely deserves a closer look.

Can vary from 10cm to 45cm tall.

LOOK FOR Rather slim, upright plants with several flowers opening in turn from the bottom up. Even when plentiful, however, Bee Orchids can be surprisingly difficult to spot until you 'get your eye in'.

WHEN TO GO In flower from early June to late July. The basal leaves appear in the winter but have largely withered by the time the flowers appear. In some years they can occur in large numbers, but in others may be quite scarce.

WHERE TO GO Almost any flowery grassland on poor, dry soils: sand dunes, road verges, commons, railway cuttings, spoil heaps and old quarries. Bee Orchids can be found in a wide range of situations and turn up in unexpected places, even on garden lawns!

SCIENCE STUFF

THE FLOWERS LOOK LIKE BUMBLEBEES AND HAVE EVOLVED TO ATTRACT BEES AS POLLINATORS BY MIMICKING THEIR SHAPE, FEEL AND SMELL – HOW CLEVER IS THAT?

The Great British Wildlife Hunt
20

Cinnabar Moth

A common, wonderfully colourful day-flying moth. The striking, stripy caterpillars blend delightfully with the colours of Common Ragwort, their food plant.

2.5cm long. The sexes are similar.

LOOK FOR An unmistakable red and black moth, often found in loose colonies. Its bright colours warn predators of the poison in its body, picked up from ragwort. Adults are easily disturbed from long grass and have a rather weak flight, usually landing again quickly. The caterpillars are conspicuously yellow and black and can cover and completely strip ragwort plants before wandering off along the ground to pupate.

WHEN TO GO Adults fly from mid May to early August, while the caterpillars hatch from late June and can be found until September.

WHERE TO GO Any Rabbit-grazed grassy place with Common Ragwort (ragwort is especially characteristic of overgrazed pasture): coastal dunes and grasslands, railway cuttings, quarries, commons and fields on dry soils. The adult moths are attracted to lights at night.

TOP TIP ★ The Cinnabar Moth can be muddled-up with another day-flying moth, the Six-spot Burnet (p.179), but that is darker, with several red spots on the wing but no red border.

Wall Barley

10

One of the world's most widespread plants, this common grass will grow happily alongside well-trodden footpaths in both town and countryside.

Up to 30cm tall. Looks like barley but without the enlarged grains.

LOOK FOR The soft feathery flower heads are noticeable, at first green, but becoming yellow once the seed is set, and then spiky as it ripens in late summer.

WHEN TO GO The first flower heads appear in May. Some plants may still be in flower in October and can overwinter, but others will be dry and yellow by August.

WHERE TO GO Common on waste ground, in rough car parks, at the foot of walls and often right beside a footpath, seemingly growing out of the pavement.

NEWS EXTRA! Not so long ago the bristly seed heads of Wall Barley were used as darts by children, as when thrown at your mates they would stick to their clothes. This does not work with some modern fabrics, however, and the custom has almost disappeared. Bring back those woolly jumpers!

The Great British Wildlife Hunt
15

Large Skipper

This small butterfly heralds the summer. It is fast flying and bolshy, the territorial males knocking other insects off their favourite perches.

Wingspan 3cm.

Female.

LOOK FOR Skippers rest with their wings in a different position to other butterflies, always with the forewings raised above the hindwings. It is the largest of the skippers, and the male has dark lines down the centre of the forewing.

WHEN TO GO Adults can be found from the end of May to late August, with a peak in early July. On warm days males will fly in search of females from mid to late morning; in the early morning and afternoon they spend more time perched and are harder to spot. They like a sunny spot close to nectar-producing plants, especially bramble.

WHERE TO GO Any open, sunny spot where the grass is left to grow tall and there are plenty of flowers, especially their favourite nectar sources, including Field Scabious, Red Campion, Ragged Robin, brambles and thistles. Check out hedgerows, green lanes, woodland rides and heaths, as well as parks and gardens (as long as there is long grass).

TOP TIP ★ Large Skipper can be confused with both Small Skipper and Essex Skipper. Look closely to see the faint chequered pattern on the hind underwing of the Large Skipper.

Common Spotted Orchid

The commonest orchid, usually with very spotted leaves, but they are hugely variable and identification can be a challenge for those not familiar with orchids.

Varies in height from 5cm to 50cm.

LOOK FOR Dense, upright spikes of flowers, occasionally solitary but often in groups and sometimes in large numbers, with a spectacular variety of shapes and colours.

WHEN TO GO In flower from mid May to early August, with the peak in June and July in the south, a little later in the north.

WHERE TO GO Flowery, grassy places, from dry grassland to marshes and wet meadows, woodland rides, old gravel pits, quarries and road verges. In fact, almost anywhere, even old industrial sites. Keep on looking, as it can colonise new areas relatively quickly.

TOP TIP ✳ The ground colour of the flower can vary from dark mauve-pink to almost white, but there are always darker loops and lines; in general the darker the ground colour, the bolder the markings. Flowers that have been mistaken for Common Spotted Orchids include Red Dead-nettle, Self-heal and Bugle, and also check out Heath Spotted Orchid (p.77).

Red Dead-nettle

Self-heal

Bugle

The Great British Wildlife Hunt • 5

Poppies

Four species of poppies are found in arable fields, all brought to Britain by Stone Age farmers. Although sensitive to herbicides, they have long-lived seeds and can reappear unexpectedly after fresh cultivation.

Common Poppy (score 5) Flowers bright red, seed pods smooth and rounded.

Long headed Poppy (score 20) Flowers orange-red, seed pods long and smooth.

Rough Poppy (score 40) Flowers pinkish-red, seeds pods round and bristly.

Prickly Poppy (score 40) Flowers blood-red, seeds pods long and slightly prickly.

WHEN TO GO Common Poppy has the longest flowering period, from June to September. The others mainly flower from June to late July.

WHERE TO GO The margins of arable fields, mostly wheat or barley on light, sandy or gravelly soils. Rough Poppy is largely confined to areas with chalk or limestone soils. Common Poppy is by far the commonest, and can be found on disturbed waste ground, indeed anywhere with freshly turned soil.

The Great British Wildlife Hunt

5

Meadow Brown

One of the most widespread and abundant butterflies, it will keep you company on any countryside walk in high summer. Look for its slow, floppy flight.

Wingspan 40–60mm

Black spots with a single white 'eye'.

Light markings can vary in size.

LOOK FOR A large brown butterfly, flying around grassy places and stopping to feed on a wide variety of common wild flowers: knapweeds, thistles and brambles. There can often be large numbers in one area. Females lay eggs on grasses and the caterpillars are green and well camouflaged; they feed at night. Late in the season many of the adult butterflies can look extraordinarily tatty.

WHEN TO GO Adults have a long flight season, from early June to late September. Early morning is a good time to see them perched and sunning themselves, while they are often the only butterflies on the wing on dull days and late into the evening.

WHERE TO GO Head for those delightful grassy places, meadows, rough fields, downland, coastal footpaths and dunes, woodland rides, hedgerows and green lanes. Meadow Browns will also visit gardens and parks of all sizes.

TOP TIP ✶ Easy to confuse with the Gatekeeper, another very common brown butterfly, but that is smaller, has much more orange in the wings and a double white 'eye' in the centre of the black spots. The 'eye spots' are thought to help distract a predator.

The Great British Wildlife Hunt
15

Common Knapweed

So common that it is sometimes overlooked, this plant is a survivor and is often found where there are few other wild flowers, thus benefiting other wildlife too.

LOOK FOR Vivid reddish-purple flowers on upright, solitary stalks up to 80cm high (although they can be much shorter.) The flowers are nectar-rich and on sunny days are usually surrounded by a selection of insects – hoverflies, butterflies and bees. Small flocks of finches feed on the seeds in autumn and winter.

WHEN TO GO In flower from June to September.

WHERE TO GO Common Knapweed is a meadow plant that has adapted to any grassy place, so look for it on road verges, field margins, hedge bottoms, footpaths, railway cuttings, grassy woodland rides and cliff-top grassland. It can be found almost everywhere except the highest mountains.

COMMON KNAPWEED

'RAYED' COMMON KNAPWEED

Greater Knapweed

SCIENCE STUFF

COMMON KNAPWEED HAS TWO DISTINCT TYPES OF FLOWERS: THE COMMON SMALL-FLOWERED FORM AND AN UNCOMMON 'RAYED' FORM THAT HAS A RING OF FORKED, EXTRA-LONG PETALS AROUND THE FLOWER. THE RAYED FORM COULD BE CONFUSED WITH GREATER KNAPWEED, A RATHER LARGER PLANT WITH DEEPLY DIVIDED LEAVES AND MUCH PALER GLOBULAR CLUSTERS OF BRACTS BELOW THE FLOWER.

The Great British Wildlife Hunt
30

Marbled White

An unmistakable large, black and white butterfly that is one of the delights of the flowery chalk downs of southern England.

LOOK FOR The only large, chequered, black and white butterfly in Britain. Adults have a definite preference for purple flowers so look for areas with Marjoram, scabiouses, thistles and knapweeds. Females may be found flying over grassy areas, laying eggs in the vegetation. On dull days look for them roosting in groups on tall grass stems, or hanging from flower heads – great for a photograph.

FIELD SCABIOUS

Quite a large butterfly, with a wingspan of 50-60mm. Females are similar to males, but have a brownish tinge to the underside of the wings.

COMMON KNAPWEED

WHEN TO GO Adults have a short flight period, from mid-June to mid-August. The best time to look is July when there can be large numbers on the wing at a colony. Arrive early in the day for a closer look at those fabulous markings, as you will often find them catching the morning sun with their wings open.

WHERE TO GO Unimproved grassland with areas of long grass and plenty of flowers. Chalk downland is the typical habitat but try also woodland rides and clearings, coastal grassland, commons and old railway cuttings.

MARJORAM

TOP TIP ★ If you visit at dusk in late May, hunt for the caterpillars feeding in the tops of grasses. By June they will have disappeared, as they pupate at ground level.

The Great British Wildlife Hunt

30

Common Broomrape

Most unlikely looking plants, often appearing to be dead. Broomrapes have no green leaves and are parasites, extracting all their nutrients from the roots of other plants.

The flower spike can be yellowish, reddish or purplish.

LOOK FOR Stocky upright plants without leaves, they often look dried-up and dead. Look closely to see the flowers packed around the stem. Broomrapes could be confused with an orchid, but their flowers have no stalk and are attached directly to the stem. The precise shape of the flower and the colour of the stamens and style help to identify the species, but often the identity of the host plant nearby is all that is necessary once you have decided that the plant is a broomrape.

WHEN TO GO In flower from June to September. The dried stems persist for most of the year.

WHERE TO GO This is the commonest broomrape, parasitic on a wide variety of other plants, most often on members of the pea family. Look for it in flowery grassland with plenty of clovers and vetches.

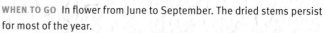

NEWS EXTRA!

All the other British broomrapes are much less widespread. These plants are parasitic on the plants that give them their names.

Ivy Broomrape

Yarrow Broomrape

Thyme Broomrape

Winter thrushes

One of the pleasures of autumn and winter is watching fields and hedgerows come alive with the chattering calls and colourful plumage of Redwings and Fieldfares.

Fieldfares are 26cm long, the same size as a Blackbird.

Redwings are 21cm long and rather slimmer than other thrushes.

LOOK FOR Large and often noisy flocks of thrushes. Fieldfares stand upright and their grey head and rump and brown wings are distinctive. They are very noisy: listen for their loud *chack-chack-chack* flight call. Redwings have a distinct whitish eyebrow, but the red in their 'wing' is actually on the flank and often hidden. Redwings give a thin *seeip* call in flight, which can even be heard after dark as they fly high overhead on migration.

WHEN TO GO Both are winter visitors from northern Europe and may be found from October to March. Their numbers increase as winter progresses but all are gone by late April.

WHERE TO GO Hedgerows, orchards, green lanes, pastures and arable fields. They prefer to be near woods or scrub, where they roost. Both species will visit large parks and gardens, sometimes in urban areas, especially in cold weather or when lots of berries are available – they quickly strip the bushes clean and move on.

TOP TIP ★ In open countryside Fieldfares and Redwings form large flocks, which may be seen moving slowly across a grassy or ploughed field searching for leatherjackets and other invertebrates.

SPECIES CHECKLIST Use these pages to record your discoveries.

SPECIES	POINTS	DATE	PLACE	RECORDER/FB
Adder **p70**	15			
Ancient tree **p20**	10			
Avocet **p148**	25			
Barn Owl **p196**	25			
Bearded Tit **p96**	25			
Bee Orchid **p203**	30			
Belemnite **p153**	25			
Bird's-nest Orchid **p43**	25			
Bird's-nest fungus **p56**	50			
Bittern **p95**	45			
Bluebell with Early-purple Orchid **p44**	15			
Bottle-nosed Dolphin **p161**	40			
Bracket fungi **p27**	15			
Brown hare **p190**	15			
Brown Trout **p120**	20			
Chiffchaff **p37**	10			
Cinnabar Moth **p204**	20			
Common and Grey Seals **p157**	25			
Common Broomrape **p212**	30			
Common Darter **p51**	10			

SPECIES	POINTS	DATE	PLACE	RECORDER/FB
Common Knapweed **p210**	15			
Common Lizard **p75**	25			
Common Spotted Orchid **p207**	20			
Cormorant **p105**	10			
Cowslip **p198**	15			
Cranberry **p82**	25			
Crested tit **p22**	30			
Cuckoo **p200**	25			
Curlew **p138**	15			
Cuttlefish bone **p146**	15			
Dark Green Fritillary **p176**	30			
Dartford Warbler **p69**	25			
Demoiselles **p115**	15			
Dipper **p101**	25			
Dodder **p83**	30			
Edible Cockle **p149**	15			
Eider **p152**	25			
Emperor Moth **p71**	40			
Enchanter's Nightshade **p52**	15			
Firecrest **p41**	40			
Fly Agaric **p64**	10			

SPECIES	POINTS	DATE	PLACE	RECORDER/FB
Frogbit p132	15			
Fulmar p156	20			
Giant Wood Wasp p49	25			
Golden-ringed Dragonfly p78	20			
Grass Snake p109	25			
Grayling p93	25			
Great Spotted Woodpecker p30	10			
Green Tiger Beetle p374	15			
Green Woodpecker p194	25			
Grey Heron p106	5			
Grey Squirrel p25	5			
Heath Milkwort p72	10			
Heath SpottedOrchid p77	10			
Hedgehog p197	35			
Hermit crab p160	15			
Herring Gull p144	5			
Holly Blue p199	20			
Jay p23	10			
Jellyfish p162	15			
Kingfisher p97	25			
Large Skipper p206	15			

SPECIES	POINTS	DATE	PLACE	RECORDER/FB
Lichens **p32**	15			
Limpet **p167**	5			
Little Owl **p191**	30			
Little Tern **p170**	25			
Long-tailed tit **p34**	10			
Longhorn Moths **p46**	25			
Marbled White **p211**	30			
Marram Grass **p139**	15			
Marsh Harrier **p98**	15			
Marsh Helleborine **p118**	25			
Marsh Marigold **p108**	10			
Marsh Orchids **p113**	15			
Marsh Samphire **p180**	10			
Mayfly **p110**	10			
Meadow Brown **p209**	5			
Mermaid's purse **p141**	20			
Minotaur Beetle **p80**	25			
Moorhen **p103**	5			
Mosses, liverworts & filmy ferns **p65**	20			
Nightjar **p76**	40			
Nut Weevil **p48**	40			

SPECIES	POINTS	DATE	PLACE	RECORDER/FB
Nuthatch p31	20			
Oak apple gall p33	15			
Oil beetle p168	50			
Otter p104	50			
Oystercatcher p134	5			
Peregrine Falcon p158	25			
Pipefish p172	35			
Polypody p35	15			
Pond Skater p112	15			
Poppies p208	5			
Puffin p263	25			
Purple Hairstreak p5 4	40			
Purple Loosestrife p121	10			
Razor Clam p164	10			
Red Fox p195	25			
Red Grouse p68	15			
Red Squirrel p24	25			
Red Wood Ant p26	10			
Redshank p151	10			
Reed Bunting p99	5			
Ringed Plover p140	20			

SPECIES	POINTS	DATE	PLACE	RECORDER/FB
Rock Pipit **p154**	25			
Roe Deer **p28**	25			
Round-leaved Sundew **p79**	15			
Sand hopper **p165**	20			
Scottish Wood Ant **p26**	10			
Sea anemones **p143**	10			
Sea Bindweed **p178**	15			
Sea Holly **p188**	20			
Sea Lavender **p181**	10			
Sea Lettuce **p150**	10			
Sea Potato **p155**	25			
Sea slugs **p159**	45			
Sea Wormwood **p145**	20			
Sea wracks **p136**	15			
Sedge Warbler **p111**	15			
Shelduck **p147**	15			
Shore Crab **p173**	15			
Short-eared Owl **p67**	35			
Silver Y Moth **p202**	20			
Silver-studded Blue **p81**	15			
Six-spot Burnet Moth **p179**	10			

SPECIES	POINTS	DATE	PLACE	RECORDER/FB
Skylark **p193**	15			
Slime mould **p55**	25			
Smooth Newt **p107**	20			
Solitary wasps **p92**	25			
Southern Hawker **p119**	15			
Sparrowhawk **p36**	15			
Speckled Wood **p38**	15			
Spoonbill **p142**	35			
Spring Squill **p169**	20			
Squat Lobster **p171**	25			
Stag Beetle & Lesser Stag Beetle **p50**	45			
Starfish **p135**	10			
Stinkhorn fungus **p57**	10			
Stoat **p192**	30			
Stonechat **p66**	15			
Swallowtail **p116**	30			
Sweet Briar **p201**	25			
Thrift **p175**	15			
Toothwort **p39**	35			
Tree Pipit **p73**	25			

SPECIES	POINTS	DATE	PLACE	RECORDER/FB
Treecreeper **p29**	25			
Turnstone **p137**	15			
Wader roost **p189**	20			
Wall Barley **p205**	10			
Wall Brown **p174**	20			
Water Mint **p133**	10			
Water Rail **p102**	35			
Water Scorpion **p100**	35			
Water Vole **p94**	35			
Whelk egg case **p166**	15			
Whirligig Beetle **p114**	10			
White Admiral **p53**	25			
Wild Strawberry **p47**	20			
Winter thrushes **p213**	15			
Witches broom **p21**	10			
Wood Sorrel **p40**	15			
Wood Warbler **p45**	25			
Woodcock **p42**	20			
Yellow Water-lily **p117**	10			
Yellow Horned Poppy **p177**	20			

Favourite walks

PLACE	DATE	TOTAL SCORE
Thursford Woods	5/5/2013	225
Local patch	6/6/2013	150
Family holiday challenge, North Wales	12–24/8/2013	300

Making your records count

The best place to start (because there are many recording schemes both national and local) is the Biological Records Centre website www.brc.ac.uk. You can then follow the links under 'recording' to find a complete list of schemes and societies that collect records and organise a wide variety of surveys. A great tool to help identify your sightings is ispot, an online 'help' site run by the Natural History Museum. This also gives links to some great online identification guides.

Don't forget to join in with The Great British Wildlife Hunt Facebook community too. Your sightings and stories can be shared with everyone. Maybe you have set yourself a challenge for a year, a holiday or just the weekend. We would love to hear about them.

Recommended reference books

Books are incredibly useful to the nature hunter: my most treasured was *Insects of Britain and Western Europe* which gave me the vast range of insects at my fingertips. Suddenly I knew exactly what sort of insect I was looking at. Many insects, as well as some plants, lichens, mosses and liverworts and fungi, cannot be easily identified right down to individual species. You may find that more specialist books are necessary to take your research further. There are societies for almost every group and these, such as The British Lichen Society www.britishlichensociety.org.uk will give you a great deal of help and guidance.

Some of my favourite books for identifying different species are:

RSPB Pocket Guide to British Birds Simon Harrap, Christopher Helm
Freshwater Life of Britain and Northern Europe Malcom Greenhalgh and Denys Ovenden, Collins
Insects of Britain and Western Europe Michael Chinery, A & C Black
Harrap's Wild Flowers Simon Harrap, Bloomsbury
Seashore Safaris Judith Oakley, Graffeg
Mammals of Britain & Europe David Macdonald Priscilla Barrett, Collins
Complete Guide to British Mushrooms and Toadstools Paul Sterry and Barry Hughes, Collins

Photo credits

K Smith; 95 t Simon Litten; 97 b Mike Lane; 98 tr David Tipling; 100 t Mike Lane; b B. Borrell Casals; 101 t Mike Lane; b Paul Hobson; 102 b Derek Middleton; 104 t Simon Litten; b Paul Hobson; 107 tl Derek Middleton; tr Martin B Withers; br Chris Mattison; 110 tl Matt Cole; bl B. Borell Casals; 112 bl Nigel Cattlin; bc Derek Middleton; br Richard Becker; 114 r Foto Natura Stock; 120 b Derek Middleton; bl Juriah Mosin; 133 Anne and Simon Harrap; 137 tr Imagebroker, Friedhelm Adam; b Erica Olsen; 140 bl Bill Coster; 147 b Wim Klomp; 151 c Hugh Clark; b Marcel van Kammen; 155 b Steve Trewhella; 156 b Steve Trewhella; 157 tr Bill Coster; 158 tr Ingo Arndt; 159 tr D P Wilson; c D P Wilson; br D P Wilson; 163 b Paul Hobson; 170 t Horst Jegen; c Heike Odermatt/Minden Pictures; 174 tr Hans Dieter Brandl; b Thomas Marent/Minden Pictures; 176 c Steve Young; b Malcom Schuyl; 190 t Simon Litten; 191 bl Martin B Withers; 193 tl Roger Tidman; 194 t Neil Bowman; 195 tr Richard Becker; 196 t Paul Sawer; b Paul Sawer; 197 b Konrad Wothe; 200 t Marcel van Kammen; tl Hans Lang; 210 t Peter Wilson; 213 l Gianpiero Ferrari; r John Hawkins; br Gary K Smith.

RSPB-images.com 6 l Steve Knell; br David Kjaer; 23 tr Malcolm Hunt; 31 t Mark Sisson; b Guy Rogers; 36 tl Steve Knell; tr Richard Brooks; 37 t Mark Sisson; br David Kjaer; 41 r David Kjaer; 45 b Steve Round; 68 b Steve Round; 69 br Mike Read; 76 bl David Tipling; 93 c David Tipling; 95 b Jeroen Stel; 97 t Mike Lane; 98 tl Richard Brooks; b Richard Brooks; 99 tl Guy Rogers; tr Tony Hamblin; 102 t Roger Tidman; 103 t Mike Read; b Mike Lane; 105 b Steve Knell; 106 t David Kjaer; c Richard Revels; 114 l Richard Revels; 119 Richard Revels; 138 tl Mike Lane; tr Ray Kennedy; bcr David Osborn; 141 c1 Graham Eaton; 148 t Edwin Kats; 151 t Guy Rogers; 152 t Mark Hamblin; bl Steve Knell; 154 t David Kjaer; b Mark Hamblin; 157 b Mike Read; 158 tl Peter Cairns; b Ben Hall; 163 t Ray Kennedy; 170 b Steve Knell; 183 t Roger Wilmshurst; b David Tipling; 191 t Peter Cairns; 193 tr Steve Round; 197 t Guy Rogers; 200 b David Kjaer.

Shutterstock.com 8 tl Bruce MacQueen; tr Utopia 88; 15 c Ermess; br Standard; 18 tl Dariush M; 22 t Mirek Srb; b BMJ; 23 tl Menno Schaefer; 25 t Aleksei Verhovski; 27 tr SW_Stock; cl Steven Belanger; 28 tl Pim Leijen; tr Harsanyi Andras; b Erik Mandre; 30 t Menno Schaefer; clb FomaA; b Sebastian Knight; 34 t Grant Glendenning; bl Menno Schaefer; 38 bl Christophe Buquet; 46 cl Alessandro Zocc; 50 tl Alexuss K; tr Henrik Larsson; tl alslutsky; 64 br Stephen Finn; 66 tl Martin Maritz; tr Antonio Guillem; 68 tl Steve Ellis; 73 b Ainars Aunins; 75 br Steve McWilliam; 88 tl Christopher Elwell; 89 tr Photoseeker; 91 t Andrew Fletcher; c1 Matt Gibson; 92 b Mike Charles; 96 t Andrew Sproule; b Florian Andronache; 104 t John A Cameron; 105 t Kenneth William Caleno; 106 b Craig Bird Photos; 109 t Neil Hardwick; b Matteo Photos; 110 tr Atila Jandi; 111 t Florian Andronache; b Menno Schaefer; 115 br Christian Mueller; 116 b Radka Palenikova; 131 tr Andy Fox Photography; bl Peter Evidge; 132 bl Juriah Mosin; 134 t David Dohnal; b David Dohnal; 137 tl Chris 2766; 138 bl Menno Schaefer; bcl Ainars Aunins; br Pim Leijen; 140 t BMJ; 142 t Mircea Bezergheanu; bl Stu Porter; br Mircea Bezergheanu; 144 t Patryk Kosmider; b Andrew Astbury; 146 c Alexandru Axon; b Little Sam; 147 t Wolfgang Kruck; 156 t Mark Caunt; 157 br Majusko95; 161 t Four Oaks; b David Nagy; 162 cr Marianne Campolongo; b Sergey Galushko ; 167 tr Ingrid Maasik; 172 b RCB Shooter; 174 tl Mark Mirror; 179 c Martin Fowler; 185 Martin Fowler; 187 t Ref: 9548315445; 188 b Zagart; 190 bl Martin Fowler; 191 br S Cooper Digital; 192 b Outdoorsman; 195 tl Menno Schaefer.

The publishers are grateful to the following individuals for permission to reproduce their photos:

David Cowles 164 b; Stephen Darbyshire 122 t; Steve Gantlett 94 tl, tr; Philip Goddard 169 t; Vince Massimo 206 tr, b; Tom Murray 165; Paul Naylor 141 b, 159 tc, 160 tr, b; Mike Page 91 c2, 125; Ian Paterson 149 tl; rgbstock © Kevin Tuck 46 b; Lisa Treadwell 27 b; Wikipedia Commons (http://en.wikipedia.org/wiki/File:Hipparchia_semele.jpg): Katja Schäfer 85 tr; Jessica Winder 150 b, 162 cl; Richard Winn 29 b; Pete Withers 71 t.

Many thanks also to Peter Fearon for his help with sourcing images of Firecrests and Steve Duckett for urban Peregrines.